HOW TO
BE A
FINANCIALLY
SECURE
WOMAN

HOW TO BE A FINANCIALLY SECURE WOMAN

Mary Elizabeth Schlayer, Ed.D.
with Marilyn H. Cooley

RAWSON ASSOCIATES PUBLISHERS, INC.

New York

Permission has been granted by Communication Channels, Inc. to use material from *Wills of the U.S. Presidents,* copyright 1976 by Herbert R. Collins and Donald B. Weaver.

Permission has been granted by G. P. Putnam's Sons, publishers, to use material from LIVING IT UP: OR THEY STILL LOVE ME IN ALTOONA, George Burns, Copyright 1977.

. . . TO CARLOS

who said "I do" many years ago
and has been doing ever since so that
I might be free for my endless projects

Acknowledgments

Our thanks to the following individuals and organizations for their help in this work:

William E. Burkhalter, *partner, Southwest General Insurance Agency;* Vernon G. Bratten, Jr., *president, Bratten Construction, Inc.;* Carnegie-Mellon University, Development Department; Raymond W. Cooley, *president, Cooley and Shillinglaw;* Jim Corbett, *Houston Home Builders Association;* Orville I. Cox, *E. F. Hutton & Co.;* Credit Bureau of Houston; Thomas Q. Davidson, *Insurance, Alexander & Alexander of TX;* Editors, *Fort Wayne* NEW PRESS; Don Pickels, *managing editor,* HOUSTON CHRONICLE; Jerome Range, *District Group Rep., Mass. Mutual Life Ins.;* Dick Reves, *automobile dealer;* Perry Smith, *Insurance Co. of North America;* Charles Saunders, *partner, Fulbright and Jaworski (Fulbright);* Henry E. Sodke, Jr., *advisor to Investment Clubs;* Dean Witter and Company; Mary Wren, *vice president, Merrill Lynch, Pierce, Fenner and Smith;* Venita Van Caspel, *president, Van-Caspel & Co., Inc., Stockbrokers.*

Contents

FOREWORD   xi

INTRODUCTION   1

   Test Your Financial Knowledge   3

1. MONEY ON THE JOB: *Making It—Keeping It*   9

   How to Make It   9
   How to Find a Job   11
   First Day on the Job   13
   Expand Your Job   14
   Salary Increases   17
   Executives   20
   Going into Business on Your Own   23
   Learn to Think Like a Professional   24
   Where Does Your Salary Go?   25
   Start Saving   26
   Quiz   26

2. MONEY OFF THE JOB: *Expanding What You Have*   29

   Building an Estate   30
   Savings Accounts   32
   Certificates of Deposit   34
   Treasuries   34
   Other Federal Bonds   38

Stock Market   39
Finding a Broker   42
How to Judge a Potential Investment   44
Mutual Funds   47
Bonds   49
Going It Alone vs. Investment Clubs   51
Collections as an Investment   52
Real Estate   53
Quiz   62

3. MONEY FOR THE REST OF YOUR LIFE: *On
   Pensions and Profit Sharing, Insurance and IRA*   66

Individual Retirement Account (IRA)   66
Life Insurance   68
Term Insurance   73
Whole or Straight Life   74
How to Check Costs, Companies, and Agents   75
Endowment   77
Annuities   77
Group Insurance   78
Health Insurance   79
Quiz   83

4. MONEY FOR TAXES   85

Tax Shelters   85
High Income—Low Deductibles   86
Watch for Deductibles   87
What to Look for in High-Risk Tax Shelters   87
A Tax Shelter Should Save Money for You   87
Quiz   87

5. THE WORLD OF MONEY: *Credit, Banks, and Loans*   89

Credit   89
Banks   97
Shop for Money   102
Kinds of Loans   103
More About Making a Loan   106
Quiz   108

6. **MONEY, LOVE, AND MARRIAGE:** *The Economics of Money When Married or Living Together*   112

   Marriage Contract and Pre-Nuptial Agreements   114
   Financial Goals   114
   Making a Budget   117
   Danger Areas   122
   Time Payments   122
   Overlooking Annual Bills   122
   Deeply in Debt   125
   Power of Attorney   127
   Contracts   127
   Quiz   128

7. **FOR ALL WOMEN, SINGLE AND MARRIED**   131

   The Master List   131
   Quiz   134

8. **WOMAN ON HER OWN:** *Special Tips for the Widow and Divorcée*   136

   If You Are Widowed   137
   If You Anticipate Divorce   138
   What You Should Receive as Part of Your Settlement   142
   Hire an Attorney   142
   Do-it-Yourself Divorce   143
   Fault–No-Fault   143
   Your Rights as a Divorcée   145
   Quiz   145

9. **YOUR OWN MONEY:** *The Dynamics of Being Single*   147

   Buying a Home   151
   Estimate All Expenses   154
   Condominium   157
   What to Look for in a House   158
   Townhouse   159
   Homeowners Insurance   161
   Capital Gains Tax   162
   When Should You Sell?   163
   What About a Car?   164

Car Insurance   168
Service and Repair   170
Quiz   172

10. MONEY FOR YOUR HEIRS: *Conserving an Estate with a Will*   175

What to Consider When Making a Will   176
Seal the Estate   184
Witnesses   184
Go to an Attorney   184
Taxes   185
Trusts   187
Update Your Will   189
Executor   190
Talk with Your Heirs   192
State Taxes   193
Phrases Often Used in Wills   193
Quiz   194

ONE LAST THOUGHT   198

INDEX   199

Foreword

This book is for the multitude of women who want to know more about money than how to spend it or how to open a savings account. It is for all those who want guidance in planning their financial futures, who do not want to see assets slip through their fingers due to lack of knowledge or preparation.

The future belongs to those who prepare. So ladies, let's prepare. This book will tell you how.

HOW TO
BE A
FINANCIALLY
SECURE
WOMAN

Introduction

Women have proved they can do almost anything a man can do short of fathering a child or tearing the New York telephone directory in half. They can be doctors, lawyers, merchants, chiefs, and if we still had tinkers they could be those too.

Yet many women have not learned to think of themselves as whole persons, competent to do whatever is necessary without leaning upon another human being. They may be experts in their fields but not know the first thing about what to do with their salaries. They're too busy with their careers to think about investment programs and money management. If they're married, they often depend upon their husbands to take care of investment programs. If single, they open a savings account or perhaps buy a Certificate of Deposit and are satisfied that they are making interest on their money. Well, they're right. They are making interest—just about enough to keep up with the rate of inflation.

If women are capable of holding top positions in every field from science to law to the arts, they're capable of *managing* their own money. They simply need to realize the importance of doing so. Making the money is important. Attaining their ambitions is important. But that's only half the battle. The other half is *working with their money to make it work for them.*

Even if they have been independent financially before marriage, many women turn money management over to their husbands, not seeming to remember that husbands have an alarmingly high casualty rate. Many of them unfortunately die or become disabled. Often a woman who has lived a comfortable life uncomplicated by financial concerns finds upon her husband's death that she doesn't have enough money on hand, enough readily available cash, to bury him. And she doesn't know how to get it.

Other husbands are casualties of wanderlust. Nobody seems to know what happens to them. Like single socks, they vanish into a netherland never to return. Their wives are left with a financial mishmash they're unprepared to sort out.

Divorces are increasing at an appalling rate. Even if a woman receives a generous settlement, she's not out of the financial woods until she learns how to manage what is now hers alone.

The difference between an old woman and an elderly lady—so goes an old saying—is money. On the assumption that women would prefer to become, in the ripeness of time, elderly ladies, I began advising them some years ago on how to manage money. It wasn't a planned project on my part. My position simply thrust me into the role. My own background was in finance and administration, with a doctorate in Administration, a masters degree in Economics, and years of practical financial experience managing my own affairs. I was a Lieutenant Commander in the Navy during World War II, married Rear Admiral Carlos M. Cardeza, now retired, and subsequently became a management consultant, author, lecturer, and regional director of the Delphian Society. My position helped me relate to thousands of women, and with my background in financial planning, it was inevitable that many of them would come to me for advice.

The problem was they came only *after* their finances were in a jumble. Time and again I helped them sort out tangled affairs, watched money go down the drain because of poor planning, saw women who should have been comfortably fixed forced to take low-paying employment or depend upon relatives for financial aid. Instead of being the beloved parents who were able to take the grandchildren off to Europe with them now and then, they were potential drains on their children's incomes in case of illness or accident.

The time they should have been helped, I realized, was not when they were weakened by money problems but when they were financially well. I was like a physician trying to cure an outbreak of typhoid which wouldn't have happened if people had been inoculated. I gave seminars telling women how to prepare financially but these were limited by geography. The vaccinations needed to be more widespread. This book is an attempt to inoculate a nation of women to keep them financially healthy.

TEST YOUR FINANCIAL KNOWLEDGE

How knowledgeable are you about financial affairs? Even if you know a great deal about some fields of finance, say credit and banking, you may know little about investments and wills. To test your overall financial knowledge, answer the following questions.

	True	False
1. It is best to pay for everything with cash and never run up bills or borrow money.	☐	☐
2. A joint checking account is the best to have because if one spouse dies the other can continue writing checks on the account.	☐	☐
3. If a man takes out a life insurance policy for $100,000 and pays the premiums, upon his death the full $100,000 is received by his beneficiary with no strings attached.	☐	☐
4. The best kind of will is a mutual will where the wife inherits everything from the husband and vice versa. When the remaining spouse dies, the estate is divided among the children.	☐	☐
5. A person should keep a will in a safe place, preferably a safety deposit box.	☐	☐
6. Investing money primarily means playing the stock market.	☐	☐
7. Everyone should have a savings account and put as much money as possible into it.	☐	☐
8. If a husband dies, his wife may continue using their joint credit cards after notifying the card companies of his demise.	☐	☐
9. If a woman with established credit needs to borrow money, she should do so only at her bank.	☐	☐

ANSWERS

1. *F.* If you pay cash for everything, you establish no credit. Nobody knows you, financially speaking. If you should have an emergency and need to borrow money, you'd have trouble doing so.

2. *F.* A joint checking account is not the best kind to have because upon a spouse's death, the account sometimes is frozen because of debts and is not accessible to the remaining spouse until the estate is settled.

3. *F.* The $100,000 does not go to the beneficiaries if he has taken out the policy and paid the premiums. It becomes part of his estate and is subject to taxes which may run very high if the estate is sizeable.

4. *F.* A mutual will is not the best because inheritance taxes are paid when the first spouse dies and again when the second spouse dies, so the estate is taxed twice.

5. *F.* A safety deposit box is the wrong place to keep a will. The box is usually sealed at the time of one's death. By the time it's opened, it may be too late to carry out some provisions of the will.

6. *F.* The stock market is only one way of investing money. There are many others, including municipal and corporate bonds, government securities, and real estate.

7. *F.* Everyone should save money, but a savings account in today's market costs the investor 2 or more percent depending upon the rate of inflation; for example, if you get 5¼ percent interest and inflation is 7 percent, you're losing 1¾ percent on your money. This is the price you pay for security.

8. *F.* If a husband dies, a credit card company closes his account. A wife is not allowed to continue using the credit cards even though their account was a joint one. She may reapply under her own name and will have to satisfy credit requirements.

9. *F.* A bank may charge more interest than some other lenders so it is not necessarily the best lender.

If you answered all the questions "false," you're exceptionally well informed. If you missed only two, you did very well and probably will never find yourself in the following real life dramas.

Tanya had her own local talk show on television. She made a good salary and was something of a celebrity in town. Her living expenses were high. She entertained a great deal, in keeping with what she considered her image. She needed an extensive wardrobe. Her hair had to be done several times a week. With one thing and another, she managed to spend most of her salary.

One afternoon on the way home from the studio, another car hit hers broadside. Her collarbone and several ribs were broken, and broken glass had cut her face. She was in the hospital a few days and then had to begin a series of plastic surgery operations to remove the facial scars.

She carried a minimum of car insurance and the other driver had none. Fortunately, she was included in medical benefits offered by the TV station but they covered only a small part of her bills. The remainder had to come out of her own pocket. The studio paid her salary for three months and then stopped. From that time on, she had no income.

She could not take permanent work because of the recurring plastic surgery but as soon as she was able, she went to work as a Kelly girl. Since she worked only part-time, her salary didn't cover her apartment rent. She had to move to a less expensive apartment in a different part of town. Her large wardrobe was unsuited for office work so she sold most of it for a fraction of its cost. She was in dire financial straits and the crowning blow came when the girl who had taken care of her props on the show took it over and made a success of it.

If Tanya had only known how to manage her money, she would have come through the financial crisis in good shape.

Another real life drama was Lydia's. Successful in her merchandising career, Lydia married for the first time in her late thirties. She continued her career, but her husband, who was an expert on stocks and bonds, took over the investment of her money. Some ten years later she learned inadvertently that she had no investments. Her husband had not invested a penny of her money. He had used it to support a mistress.

Then there's Jennifer, and there are many Jennifers in this world. She stopped working before her first child was born and never returned to outside employment. For twenty years she was involved with rearing children and homemaking. Even after the children left home, her life was closely connected with theirs as they married and had children.

When Jennifer was fifty-five, her husband died unexpectedly. She hadn't concerned herself with financial matters other than her own spending money for more than thirty years. Suddenly she was faced with total responsibility for her finances. She discovered she had a smallish joint checking account, a larger joint savings account, a house that was mortgaged, two cars (one paid for), some stock that her husband once told her about but she couldn't remember the details, her husband's life insurance policy, and his will, which left everything to her. She also found that her husband's business debts amounted to far more than the checking and savings accounts combined.

How was she going to pay the business debts? How was she going to pay for the funeral and burial? How could she find out about the stock? How much of the insurance policy was paid to her and when? How was she going to make the next house payment? And car payment? How could he have left her when she needed him so much?

Impossible scene? Not at all. It's much less grim than many of the situations that widows face.

Until he died, Jennifer's husband had gone to some lengths to cherish and protect her—but he didn't prepare her. He took care of the family budget, let her use his credit cards, gave her extra money when she was overdrawn at the bank, and generally encouraged her to be ignorant about finances.

Women tend to adopt a psychological cutoff point when it comes to money. They know how to take advantage of bargains. They may know how much money is in the savings account. But mention insurance, interest rates, investments—they don't really want to know about such things. They think probably they should learn—sometime.

Many women have been taught since they were children that one simply doesn't talk about money. This attitude carries over into adult life and inhibits a woman's thinking.

Sometimes husbands discourage their wives' interest in money matters. They may consider family financial affairs solely their responsibility.

Even if you are part of a couple, you are married not only in the eyes of God but in the eyes of the state, financially. Marriage is a legal contract forming a partnership between two people. A couple needs to recognize that they have entered into, among other things, a business arrangement.

Since it is a business arrangement, both partners should be fully aware of all the business concerned. Together, they should participate in a review of the status of their "business" not less than once a year. Every six months would be better, but that's probably too much to hope for. A good time for the review is income-tax time.

Single women should also review their financial status at least once a year—list everything they own, stocks, bonds, bank accounts along with their approximate values. They should know how much has come in since the last review and how much has gone out.

Until a woman knows where she stands, she can hardly know where she's going. So she must know her position and the direction in which she wants to head.

WHAT ARE YOUR GOALS?

Once you know where you are, it's time to determine specific goals. Know what you want to achieve. How can you accomplish anything if you don't know what you want to accomplish?

Decide now on an objective. What is your financial goal?

When you think about goals, you'll probably find you have one for this year or next, another for someday and an ultimate aim for your old age. For instance you may want to buy a house. Or you may want a larger house. A couple of children can reduce the size of a dwelling as effectively as a bulldozer pushing in the walls. Or maybe you haven't had a real honest-to-goodness vacation in a while and you want to go to Europe. Houses and European vacations cost a lot of money so you have to plan in order to afford them.

Your someday goal could be almost anything. One of my friends is a super cook whose dream is to open her own restaurant and serve gourmet food to people who appreciate it. An artist may want her own gallery and an antiques buff her own shop. Most people have to wait many years for these dreams to materialize.

In talking to people I find there comes a time in the thinking of both women and men when they suddenly realize that someday has arrived. Maybe all their lives they've been thinking, someday I'll get a whatever, or someday I'll go somewhere, or someday I'll do such and such. One day they think, I've waited long enough. It's time to get or go or do. Someday is now. You must plan properly so that you can afford your someday when you're ready.

To make the whole thing more realistic, get some paper and a pencil. Once your thoughts are down in black and white, they become more real than amorphous questions floating around in your mind.

Make a list of your goals. List the costs, of course. How can you plan realistically for something if you don't know how much it's going to cost? If your ultimate financial goal is retirement with a decent income, you may be unable to pick an exact figure since taxes and inflation undoubtedly will cause changes over the years. But do the best you can and adjust the figure as necessary in the future.

Your list of goals may look something like this:

	Necessary Annual Income
As Soon As Possible buy home	$20,000
Someday travel and buy country home	$45,000
Ultimately quit work, move to country home	$20,000

Now you know what you want, approximately when you want it, and approximately how much it's going to cost. Include these figures in your annual budgeting, which I discuss later at more length. When you start putting money aside for a specific thing, you're a giant step closer to your goal.

Financial planners are fond of saying, "No one ever plans to fail, they just fail to plan." It's never too late to start. It's also never too early to start.

You need to start today.

The first step is acquiring the money.

Money On the Job

Making It—Keeping It

A woman has three legal ways of acquiring money—she can inherit it, marry it, or earn it. Inheriting requires the least effort on your part and if you happen to be an heiress, congratulations. Most of us aren't, unfortunately, so we have the options of marrying it, earning it, or doubling our odds by doing both.

So let's start at the beginning of your financial career and discuss making money.

HOW TO MAKE IT

Whether you're twenty or fifty, single or married, mother or childless, the basic steps toward felicitous employment are much the same. The first thing to do is clarify your goals. Why do you intend to work?

People work for three and a half reasons:

1.   They have a specific ambition they want to achieve
1½.   They enjoy the work itself

2. They want to make money
3. They have time on their hands and nothing else to do

The number three group may be young women planning to marry and marking time in the interim, married women planning to quit and have children within a few years, or older married women whose children have grown and left home. These women rarely aim at important jobs. They tend to choose jobs where working conditions are pleasant and the salary satisfactory.

The first category, those who have specific ambitions, go into particular fields. The money they earn is secondary. Their primary goal is fulfillment of ambition.

Some lucky people work because that's what they like to do!

But the vast majority of us aren't sure what we want to do. We know we've got to support ourselves and drift almost casually into one field or another simply because a job was open at the time we needed it. This way of going about your career requires the least effort on your part—but probably provides the least reward.

If you're going to work to make money primarily, you need to consider two major things. First, how can you make the most money? If that's your purpose in working, you may as well do the best you can.

Second, once you find the highest paying jobs, you must decide if you're suited to them. Many sales jobs, for instance, pay well but many people are unsuited to selling. A shy introvert would rather work for a pittance in a job where she's secure than make $100,000 calling on strangers all day. A hearty extrovert on the other hand would take a low-paying sales job which enabled her to be around people rather than spend her days huddled over records in an office.

Most people are a combination of introvert-extrovert to one degree or another. If you don't know which you are, think whether you prefer working with people or by yourself. An extrovert is happier involved with other people. Introverts are happier doing a job which is primarily their own responsibility and depends little upon other people's contributions. For instance if you want to be an attorney and you're an extrovert, you may make a good trial lawyer. If you're an introvert, you'll probably be happier doing corporate work or even research for the trial lawyer.

Choose the type of work you'll be happy doing regardless of your motivation for working. You'll be healthier and do better work if you *look forward* to going to work each morning, or night, instead of dreading it. I knew a young woman who had studied to be a dentist and built a lucrative practice before she discovered she simply didn't like putting her fingers into people's mouths all day. She was so unhappy that she suffered nausea and vomiting each morning before she went to work. Obviously, the faster she could get out of it, the better.

If you don't know where you'd be happy, take an aptitude test. Most high schools, colleges, and business schools offer them. Or you may be able to arrange for one through an employment agency.

Perhaps you have two goals in working. You may want not only to support yourself but to develop a social life through your work. If that's part of your motive for working, check out the possibilities before interviewing. How many people of which sexes are employed at the job you're considering and how old are they? Don't bury yourself in an office of sixty-year-old men even if the salary is fantastic. Look instead at a field that attracts people like yourself or engineers, salesmen or technicians.

If you have a specific field you want to work in, don't overlook any entry into it. For instance I know a publisher who advertised for a secretary. Among the several female applicants was a lone man, a recent college graduate with a very high scholastic record. He had been offered other jobs with attractive titles but none in the industry he wanted to enter. He explained he wanted to learn the publishing field and this seemed the best way to learn everything about it, no matter what the title. He was right. He made a success of the job and subsequently moved into a position he could never have hoped to acquire without the experience he gained as a secretary.

HOW TO FIND A JOB

Once you've decided which field you want to be in and have the necessary training, you're ready to start looking for a job. About 80 percent of vacancies are filled by personal recommendation. Many business and technical schools try to find job openings for their students. So do some colleges. If you have neither an individual nor a school to recommend you, don't despair. The classified sections of newspapers are filled with Help Wanted ads. Employment agencies are eager to place new applicants. You can pick agencies from the phone book or from Help Wanted ads in the papers.

Phone first. Tell them your job qualifications and ask if they have suitable openings.

Be realistic in looking for a job. I meet young people who expect to graduate from college and move immediately into a top executive position. This is not being realistic. Even if you were a straight A student, you still need experience before you can handle an important job.

If you're returning to work after some years at home, don't expect to move back into the position you had before. Times and methods change very rapidly and the job you had may now be done by a computer. If you have been away from work awhile, visit your old company, if possible, and see if they're still doing things the way you did them.

Eventually you'll go for an interview with a prospective employer. Be prepared to tell him or her the amount of salary you want. If you're in doubt about how much you can expect to earn, check ads in the newspaper and ask employment agencies. If the prospective employer asks how much you want, tell him with no quibbling and hedging. I've heard employers complain that many applicants when asked about salary answer they have to earn a particular amount to meet their expenses. Every employer I've talked with has been irritated by this answer. An employer is interested in what you can do for his company and how much you're going to cost him. (Are you interested in how much it costs him to run his firm? Probably not. You're interested in how much you can earn.) So don't tell him you *need* to earn a specific amount. Tell him how much you expect and think you are worth monetarily.

How much you're worth to a company is not always easy to determine. If you're going into a standard position, such as secretary, bookkeeper, teacher, sales clerk, clothing buyer, nutritionist, nurse, office manager, you should have no difficulty learning what similar positions pay. If you're going into a selling job, you may be offered a base salary and a percentage of commission on your sales. In this case your own selling efforts will determine your income.

If you're going into public relations, marketing, decorating, private nursing, or some other area where salaries are less well defined, you have more leeway with the amount of salary you may expect. Try to find out from friends and employment agencies what similar jobs pay. Try to estimate what your services will be worth to the company or individual. How much can you expand the company's business or improve its image? A good public relations person working for a public utility—half the country is angry with utility companies—can be worth her weight in gold. Private nurses or companions for the elderly are worth a great deal to relatives of the patient. The more confident you are of your ability to do a good job, the more you can ask.

If the prospective employer agrees with your figures, fine. If he doesn't, what then? So many variables have to be considered that it's impossible to give an answer that will hold good in all cases. For instance:

- How experienced and capable are you?
- What's the job market like? Are jobs easy to come by or are many people out of work?
- How many openings are there for your particular skills?
- How badly do you need work?
- How much opportunity does this job offer for learning and progressing in your chosen field?

You must consider all these factors before deciding whether or not to come down on your salary requirements.

If you and your employer aren't too far apart in amount, you might agree to begin at his price with the promise of raises every three months until you reach your amount. Or you might offer to work at his figure for six months with the agreement that at that time he meet your price.

FIRST DAY ON THE JOB

Let's assume that you and your employer agree on the amount of salary and you come to work Monday morning. Here are a few do's and don'ts for the job.

DO   learn your work as rapidly as possible. You're worth next to nothing until you can do the job you were hired for.

DO   move briskly and energetically in the office instead of strolling about.

DO   express concisely what you want to say.

DO   ask questions when necessary but don't pester others with questions about your work if you can help it.

DO   keep your voice clear but low. Never talk loudly or laugh boisterously at the office or any other public place.

DO   confine romancing to after-work hours even if you date someone in the organization.

DON'T   take long coffee breaks and lunch hours. Don't be late and don't leave early. Don't take off more than you must for personal reasons.

DON'T become involved in office gossip. The others may consider you peculiar but you'll be better off in the long run.

DON'T bring personal problems into the office.

DON'T spend a lot of time on the telephone. When you're at work, the job comes first.

Here's an important one for young, inexperienced women:

DON'T expect every hour or even every day of work to be stimulating and exciting. Every now and then I meet a young woman who tells me she's unhappy with her job. She spent a lot of time and money training for it but now she finds it's not what she likes. When I try to find out what she doesn't like about her work, she usually winds up telling me it's boring. Believe me, I've never heard of an occupation that didn't have its dull as well as its stimulating side.

EXPAND YOUR JOB

About the time you get to know your work, you may decide you're ready to move up. But stay on where you are for a while. It's the least you can do in return for your training period. At the same time be working toward either a promotion or expansion of your position. Expansion is a sort of shifting around and spreading out to make more room for yourself instead of moving to another chair, and it's as good, sometimes better, than a promotion.

Begin the expansion process by taking on tasks that belong to someone else, not someone on a lower echelon than you but someone on a higher echelon. For instance, Mrs. Dailey was production manager in an advertising agency. The secretary-receptionist, Diane, began doing tasks that normally fell to production. She familiarized herself with the art work, knew where to find it and where to put it away. She began filing publicity releases and photographs. She learned enough about particular projects so she could talk with printers and artists when the production manager was away.

Mrs. Dailey was delighted. She had more than she could handle, and she was very pleased to find someone who was bright enough and interested enough to assume some of the work. Also, she was not afraid of competition.

Fear of competition is something you may encounter in trying to expand your position. Some persons are so possessive of their responsibilities that they look with suspicion upon anyone who offers to help them. If you run into this attitude, try to let the individual concerned know you don't want her job but that your own work load permits you to help. If this doesn't work, you have to do an end run and start doing tasks for your superior's superior. This requires tact and a certain amount of sneakiness but it's justified if your immediate superior is willfully blocking your ambitions.

You will have to arrange to be in the office with the bigger boss when your immediate superior is out—early, late, whenever. A conversation might go something like this.

YOU: Good afternoon, Miss Greer. I've been wondering how you like the new employees' newsletter.

MISS GREER: (*blank look*) I didn't know we had an employees' newsletter.

YOU: (*refraining from saying that your superior should have shown it to her*) Oh, yes, we're on our third issue. Everyone seems to enjoy it. People get to know each other better with something like this. I have a copy here.

MISS GREER: It looks interesting. Who's doing it?

YOU: I am. I get the information at lunchtime and coffee breaks and type it up at night. We did this at the last place I worked and it seemed good for company morale.

MISS GREER: Yes, I can see how it would be. So Marta was your profile person last issue. (*Marta holds an even higher position than Miss Greer.*)

YOU: Yes. I was wondering if you would be our profile person this week.

MISS GREER: I suppose so. Yes, I'd be happy to. . . . (*later*) This shows a great deal of initiative on your part. I've talked with Marta and some of the others about you and the newsletter. It isn't fair for you to do it on your own time. How would you like to make it longer and spend the majority of your time on it? You would work directly for me. It would mean an increase in salary and we'll have to think of a suitable title.

You also need to look ahead and see what's likely to happen with your company. A friend of mine holds an executive position with a firm and, knowing the business inside and out, she realized the company probably would amalgamate with another, male-oriented company, and, in the ensuing squeeze, as a woman she would lose out.

My advice to her was to create a place for herself within the company that only a woman could fill. Such positions exist in some firms and can be created in others. For instance a bank may have a woman who advises only women depositors.

Another friend created a new place for herself in her company, a savings and loan firm. She liked to travel and one day, when musing about how she would prefer to be in Jamaica instead of her office, she thought of a new public relations promotion. Why couldn't the company start a travel club offering charter trips? Further, why shouldn't she be in charge of the trips?

She kept the idea to herself until she'd worked out all the details. She priced flights and hotel accommodations at different places, figured the cost of an advertising campaign, estimated how much the company could make from new depositors who would start saving money with this firm so they could join the travel club. When she had everything together, she went directly to the president. He thought it was a great idea, gave her a substantial salary increase, and made her director of the new travel club.

It was going to be more work than she'd had before but she thought the new position was worth it. Many people want to make large salaries but few want to accept responsibilities. They say they don't want a job they can't leave at the door of the office at 5 P.M. I've rarely seen a job worth having that a person didn't take home with him. Not that you should worry about your work. You shouldn't worry about anything. Think about it, plan for it, make decisions about it, but don't spin your mental wheels by worrying. Actually when people say they don't want to take a job home with them, they usually mean they don't want work with so much responsibility that they have to think about it either on the job or off.

If you're willing to accept responsibility and are interested in your work, you'll rapidly make yourself invaluable. Don't get cocky about it. Don't think you're so nifty you can't be replaced. Almost no one is that good. But if you can say, "Yes, Mrs. Jones, I will see that this letter goes out before I leave work tonight," and do it, Mrs. Jones will be gratified to have found someone on whom she can rely.

Don't say you can do a job if you can't, of course. Saying you'll perform a task that you're unable to handle is worse than refusing in the first place. But taking on a job and carrying it through to completion can mean a great deal to your employer—and therefore, to you.

For instance I have a friend who wanted to work part-time but she simply couldn't keep herself from doing what needed to be done. She was so responsible and so good at her work in an office supply store that she received several salary increases, the store began sending her on buying trips, and eventually they talked her into working full-time. Some people are constitutionally unable to do less than their best.

Don't Be Anonymous

A woman who wants to get ahead will have to plan her own strategy for visibility. People should know her name and her capabilities.

A friend whom I'll call Joan had to take time off from work because her mother was terminally ill. She was away from the office three weeks and was concerned about her job, thinking they might decide to fire her because of her lengthy absence. Instead she was welcomed back with open arms. Her employer was sympathetic to her problem, reassuring about her job, and from that day on, couldn't seem to do enough for her. He even brought back little gifts when he went on trips. She came to the conclusion that until she was gone, he hadn't realized how much of the work load she carried. When he did, he wanted to make sure he kept her.

Your job is to make sure your employer knows how much you do without leaving for three weeks. If you've done something out of the ordinary, tell your employer. If you've had particularly good results with a customer or client, tell him or her about it. If you've pushed up sales figures, show them to your boss.

An employer may not notice your good work but is very likely to notice bad work or bad work habits such as taking off early. This is a minor form of cheating. It's piddly, like stealing stamps, and identifies you as a person who feels her interests are apart from the company's. They may be, but if you want to make points with your employer, you won't show it. You must call attention to the good, positive things you do.

Get to know your employer's likes and dislikes. Little things are important as they are in any relationship. Your employer will have pet peeves. I know a woman who gets uptight if coffee is left in the office pot at night because she feels too much has been made and the company is wasting money, which of course, it is. If your employer has pet projects, show interest in them. Ditto about personal hobbies.

Another way of gaining visibility is to work outside the company in a charitable organization. If you're active, your fellow workers will hear about it. If you hold an important office in the organization, the resulting publicity will reflect well upon both you and your company.

SALARY INCREASES

Once you've learned to do your work well and have become an asset to the company, it's time to ask for a raise. Make this a businesslike situation. Tell your employer you want to talk with him or her and make an appointment. Some people recommend that you try to keep the appointment in a conference room instead of your employer's office so you get him away from his own turf. That's trying to overcome the superiority-inferiority relationship so the two of you are on equal levels. Psychologically I suppose this is a good ploy if you anticipate a great deal of resistance about the raise. On the other hand when you tell your employer you want to talk to him, he knows you're either going to ask for a raise, tell him you're leaving, or some other momentous event, so if he's going to resist, his defenses will be up wherever the meeting is held.

Tell your employer you think you deserve a raise and why. A conversation might go something like this.

"I've been with the company six months now, Mrs. Gray. I think I've been doing satisfactory work."

She may say, "Yes, quite satisfactory." Or she may nod. Or she may simply look at you, which can be unnerving, but don't let it throw you. You continue:

"I've been doing some extra work, writing letters for Miss Hall and I've cleaned out her correspondence files, so I feel that I'm worth more to the company than I was. Therefore I'd like an increase in salary."

Mrs. Gray may say, "I've been aware of your extra work, Marcia, and I'm pleased to see you take an interest in the firm, but you must realize that when you came to work, you were worth actually far less than we paid you. It took you several months to merit the salary you were receiving since the first three months were something of a training period. So I think we should wait a few more months before considering a raise."

"I understand the first three months were a training period. However, I did answer the telephone during that period and carried on all the secretarial duties assigned me, so I feel I earned my salary. I've estimated how much a secretary for Miss Hall would earn and since I'm doing many of the duties she would do, I think I'm worth more than I'm receiving."

"But you see, we don't plan to hire a secretary for Miss Hall."

"Surely she's worth more to the company if she's out selling than in the office filing or typing letters."

"She's always been able to manage both, although her time certainly is more valuable selling than doing secretarial work. Let me think about this, Marcia, and talk to Miss Hall. Let's get together again next week."

Getting a raise probably won't be this hard. Your employer probably will say yes or no fairly quickly. If it's no, start looking for another job.

Suppose you add a new skill to your abilities. Approach your employer with notes ready to supply facts and figures.

"Miss Dalton, I'd like to talk with you about a salary increase."

"You had an increase quite recently, didn't you? About four months ago?"

"Yes, four months ago. At that time I was taking a photography course. I've been practicing at night and on weekends, and Mrs. Thompson has sent me on some photo assignments during the past month."

"I believe she said something about that. But the company likes to give raises at six-month intervals."

"I understand that, but I have been doing quite a bit of extra work. Some of the shots have to be taken at night and I had to spend most of one Saturday at a real estate development."

"I'm sure Mrs. Thompson would have called one of the freelance photographers if she had known you didn't want to work overtime."

"I don't mind working overtime and I love the photography. But I do think I should be paid for it. I've averaged the charges of the different photographers we use, and kept a log of the time I spent on the different assignments. I've saved the company at least $400 during the month."

"That much? I'd be interested in seeing your figures."

"I have them here. You see, the average freelance charge is $35 an hour. I worked a total of 15 hours on assignments. That amounts to $525. We still had to have the negatives processed and prints made commercially but that's relatively minimal, probably under $100."

"Yes, if your figures are correct—"

"I was very careful with them. Would you like me to get the exact charges for processing and printing?"

"That won't be necessary. What about your regular work? Have you managed to stay up with it and do the photography too?"

"Yes, although, as I said, I've worked some overtime."

"The figures do indicate that you're saving the company money. Of course, we couldn't give you a large raise at this time but perhaps we should work out something. I'll discuss it with Mrs. Thompson."

Figures are difficult to argue with. If you can present evidence to show you're saving a firm money, any employer will be impressed— not only with the savings but with your initiative, ambition, and ability. Here's one more example of how you can make yourself more valuable to your employer in order to receive a raise.

"Dr. Taylor, I talked with your accountant this morning and she said your rate of bills paid had increased 15 percent in the past two months."

"That's the best news I've heard today. Did she want to talk with me?"

"No. Actually I called her and asked if there had been an increase. You see, I've been conducting my own research project."

"Oh?"

"For the past three months, I've gone through the records of persons with bills two months and longer overdue, and telephoned them. I've been very polite and just reminded them that they still owed for treatments. I've tried to contact four each day."

"Is that a fact? Did I ask you to do that?"

"No. I did it on my own."

"That was very enterprising of you, Karen. I'm impressed. Darned good idea, too. You know, I think you should share in my increased income. How much are you making now?"

"I started at $600 a month."

"Let's make it $650. You deserve it."

"Thank you, Doctor."

"And keep up the good work."

EXECUTIVES

If you're aiming at being an executive within a large organization, you need special advice. You must be ambitious, intelligent, competent, and well groomed. You're not the kind of person who'll be satisfied as a secretary, bookkeeper, or even sales person of the year. You intend to get to the top.

Let's say you're twenty-five, a good age to get a foot on the ladder. During the next ten years, you'll be shopping around for a firm which is right for you. You may make several moves. Don't let yourself be stuck in any one job between the ages of twenty-five and thirty-five. Stay a year and a half to two years and, if you're not promoted, move —always to something better.

Never make a lateral move—one that neither improves your position nor your salary—no matter how difficult working conditions are or how unreasonable your employer. Hang in there until you can make a move for the better. Your goal is to have a substantial increase in salary or a better position *every two years*.

Another way to the top is piggy-backing—picking out an obviously rising executive and giving aid and assistance to him or her in the upward climb. In return you can expect to ride along to the top as your candidate's assistant.

Be wary of taking a job as secretary in hopes of moving into an executive position. It works sometimes; more often, it doesn't. If you're a good secretary, your employer won't want to lose you and so won't promote you. Increase your salary, yes. Let you get away, no.

Many long-time secretaries have even trained their new employer when the old one left. Actually the secretary should speak up for herself in these situations. She's probably more qualified for the job than most of the applicants but management may never have thought of her as a possibility. She must make her ambitions known if she doesn't want to remain a secretary all her life.

Keep looking for a company where your ambitions can be realized. You want to find a firm to which you can be loyal, one whose interests can be identified with yours. If you plan to rise to the top, you've got to feel positively toward your firm. Its well-being is your well-being.

What Is Expected of An Executive?

You'll be working on an equal basis with men so you'll be expected to do the same things. You may be required to travel. Business travel simply isn't the same as vacationing. Being stuck a couple of nights in a strange town where you have no friends can be dreary. If you have a family at home, traveling can present problems, so work it out in advance.

You may be expected to do business entertaining in the evenings. This sounds like great fun, eating at the best restaurants on an expense account. But about the third time you have to go to dinner and sparkle after a long, hard day, when your hair needs doing and your spirit needs peace and quiet, you find it's not such fun after all.

One of the major requirements for an executive is taking care of the work that is her responsibility regardless of the hours it takes. Working weekends is no fun but there is a certain status in having a job of such importance that you're needed in the office on Saturday.

Make inquiries about any executive training courses that may be available through your company and let it be known that you are willing and eager to take such a course.

Read voraciously—newspapers, magazines, advice on your work, and on finance. You can't read too much in your specific and general field.

A potential executive must make friends of fellow workers along the way, regardless of their positions. You can't have too many friends, and one enemy within an organization is too many.

About the age of thirty-five, it's time to stop job shopping and settle down with the company of your choice where hopefully you can work yourself to the summit. Learn your company's aims and policies and be prepared to promote them.

A word of advice: never get yourself in the position of competing with younger men and women. You must stay ahead of your competition. You do this by continuing to rise within your organization once you become an executive. You must stay one rung ahead of younger persons on the executive ladder.

By the time you're forty-five, if you haven't made executive level, you probably won't in a large company. There are exceptions, but very few. However with an outstanding record you may still rise to the top in a small firm.

High Paying Industries

Highest-paid executives are in the following fields:

- appliances
- autos
- chemicals
- department stores
- steel
- textiles

Lowest Paying Industries

Lowest-paid executives are in the following fields:

- air transport firms
- banks
- life insurance companies
- meat packing firms
- public utilities
- railroads

Personal Requirements for an Executive

REQUIREMENTS	TEST YOURSELF
Accuracy	How good am I at finding and correcting errors?
Good judgment	Are my decisions usually thoughtful rather than impulsive?
Follow through	Do I usually see a job through and do the implied as well as the specific assignments?
Resourcefulness	Do I usually try various possibilities until I solve a problem?
Initiative	Do I often initiate action in my group?

Consideration	Do I often do kind things without being asked?
Tact	Do I avoid ruffling the feelings of others?
Discretion	Do I refrain from divulging business and personal information?
Loyalty	Do I enthusiastically support my company and its policies?
Objectivity	Can I look at personal situations without involving my emotions?

GOING INTO BUSINESS ON YOUR OWN

All sorts of opportunities are open for women who have a particular interest or skill which they can expand into a business. I've known women who became so good at crafts such as découpage or building miniature furniture that they wound up spending full time at it and selling their wares to department stores.

Artists may decide to open their own galleries to market their paintings. Outstanding cooks may open a catering service or restaurant. Hair stylists may open their own salons. Health food enthusiasts may open stores. I heard recently of two young women who began designing their own tennis dresses. The outfits were so admired that the couple began making them on special order.

Many women buy and renovate houses. Usually they take it one house at a time. They look for a good buy, usually a house that is rundown so the price is low. It's located, however, in a good or growing neighborhood. They make structural repairs where necessary, often install new plumbing, update kitchens and baths, decorate tastefully, and put the house on the market. They usually move into the house when it's ready so they avoid paying for two dwellings at one time, and they're not particularly concerned whether the house requires two weeks or two years to sell. They're watching for another good buy.

A young literary agent I know originally worked for a publisher, so friends began bombarding her with manuscripts. If her publisher didn't like them she took them to other publishers as a personal favor to the friend. Finally she decided to make her work official and opened a literary agency along with a friend who'd had much the same experience.

I even know women who do yard work. My lawn in Florida is maintained by a young woman with a college degree who wanted to get away from city life. She brings her two preschool children along and they play while she mows and trims the grass. She has as many regular customers as she can handle and a waiting list of persons who want her to do their lawns.

Before opening a business, a woman should remember that not only is she going to have to do her work, but she's going to have to deal with taxes, and perhaps employees, which means record keeping for the government, and perhaps suppliers, which takes more record keeping. She should make sure she has time for the associated duties because if she expects to fit them into her regular working day, she'll find herself working far into the night.

If she's married, she'll want to discuss with her husband what their income-tax situation is and what it could become if her business makes money. He also should be prepared for the fact that her work is going to be important and possibly more time consuming than his. If he's going to fuss about the lack of time she spends with him or get uptight if a button falls off his shirt, they'll save a lot of hassling if they make some rules before the button ever unravels.

I won't go into detail about how to open a business. Whole books are written on the subject and if you're thinking of going into business, you'll want to read them. But I did want to mention some of the possibilities and a few of the hazards you may encounter.

LEARN TO THINK LIKE A PROFESSIONAL

Rule number one—time is money. Use your time as effectively as possible. Even if your favorite department store is having a fantastic sale and normally you'd be there when the doors open, now that you're a career person, forget it. So you'd save ten or twenty dollars. If you're gone from work, you could lose much more than that in business or in goodwill from your employer.

Grocery shopping also can be a time waster. If you're fortunate enough to have a grocery store where you can order by phone, do so. You may pay more but you'll save time that can be put into work, into self-improvement such as study, or into simply resting.

Christmas and other gift buying can be handled through department store catalogs. The store will even wrap and mail gifts, which can save you hours and hours of work.

Another major time consumer is errand running. Avoid errands whenever possible.

I don't mean you shouldn't attempt to save money but do it in the proper perspective. Put first things first. Figure out what you make per hour and what you plan to make next year. Now figure out how much time you spend running errands, buying groceries, shopping for clothes and gifts, waiting to have appliances, cars, shoes, handbags repaired. Would it be to your advantage to ignore sales, even though you pay more, so you can spend more time at what you do best—your work?

How much time did you spend the last time you went to a doctor? If it was longer than thirty minutes, the wait probably cost you money. Try to schedule doctor appointments either first thing in the morning (as he arrives), just before the doctor's lunch, or just before he leaves the office in the afternoon. Even the most conscientious physician usually manages to get out of his office in time for lunch or home-going, barring major emergencies.

Another way to save time *and* money is by watching for perks available through your company. You may be entitled to the use of a dinner or country club. You may rate a company car. When you travel you may be able to use a particular hotel or apartment which your company maintains for its executives. You may be able to combine a business trip with a vacation.

Investigate any opportunities your firm offers for buying into the company, for pensions, or for deferred salary payments that will reduce your income tax. I discuss these at length in another chapter but keep them in mind when you choose a company with which to settle.

WHERE DOES YOUR SALARY GO?

Ten percent goes to you. No matter why you're working, take 10 percent of your salary after taxes and save it for your investment program. This is your looking-to-the-future money and is important whether you're twenty or sixty years old.

This money is yours to keep, not to spend. It must not be less than 10 percent because these savings will have children in the form of interest and those children will have children.

A good part of your money during early working years probably will be spent on your appearance and self-improvement courses. You needn't feel frivolous about this. Your appearance is important whatever your career aims. Good packaging often sells the product. Unless you're already on an executive level, you don't need designer dresses and handmade shoes. But make sure you look like the kind of woman your employer would be proud to introduce to the most important customer, client, or relative.

You can save money in other ways. For instance, lounging clothes, party dresses, and novelty coats can be bought for 20 percent of what they cost new at a good resale shop.

In the chapter on budget, I discuss other ways of saving money. One of the biggest ways is to do without a car if you're in a city where that is practicable. Even if you live in an auto-oriented city like Los Angeles or Houston, you may be able to save on transportation by locating your home close to your work or vice versa, by participating in carpools, and by limiting shopping to once each week or even once each two weeks. By limiting shopping, you also save time.

If you're young and still living with your parents, don't be too eager to move into your own apartment. It has its advantages, true. It also has disadvantages. You spend more time maintaining your own apartment than you would your room at home. Besides, you spend less money at home even if you pay board.

START SAVING

Start saving with your first paycheck. If your first paycheck came long ago, start with the next one. Make a sign for yourself and put it in a prominent position on your mirror where you put on make-up each morning. This sign should read

START

Start saving 10 percent of your paycheck immediately. In a later chapter I discuss where to store your savings. For now the important thing is to *Start* saving 10 percent.

Do it with a positive attitude. Say by this time next month or two months or three months from now, depending upon your amount of salary, "I will have saved $100." Know you're going to do it. A positive attitude toward your money is as important as it is toward your job.

Now let's review some of the primary points in this chapter. See how many questions you can answer before checking the answer that follows. Good luck and may you have successful careers!

QUIZ

1. My real ambition is to be conductor of a symphony but since I have to support myself, this aim seems unrealistic. Therefore I intend

to concentrate my career on making the most money I can. Should I go into sales?

That depends upon your personality. If you enjoy dealing most of the time with people and if you're optimistic and persuasive, you may enjoy sales. If you are uncomfortable with strangers, look elsewhere.

2. Suppose I decide to pursue my ambition to be a music conductor, but the only job I can get which is even vaguely related is girl friday for the symphony director. Should I take the job?

By all means. You'll learn a great deal about the practical workings of a symphony which probably will benefit you in your climb toward becoming a conductor.

3. I don't like to talk about money. I wouldn't know how to tell a prospective employer what salary I want.

It's very easy. You simply say "I want to earn $1,000 a month" or whatever salary you have in mind. Try practicing at home in front of the mirror. Remember, your work deserves payment. You're asking for something you will earn. By determining and naming the salary you want, you're approaching your work in a professional manner.

4. I asked for $800 a month but my employer said she could only pay $650, and I took the job. I felt that I was giving in too easily but I've had very little experience and jobs of this sort are hard to find.

You probably did the right thing. When you've had more experience, you'll have more bargaining power with your employer.

5. I had a good position when I quit work 12 years ago. Now I'm having trouble finding the same kind of job even though I'm better qualified than the people who replaced me.

Don't expect to find the same kind of job when you return. Time and technology move rapidly. Take a different position and set out to prove yourself a second time.

6. I have little chance of getting a promotion because of the way our office is organized. But I like the company and don't want to leave.

Set about expanding your job. This way you can increase your salary without receiving a promotion.

7. Recently I was passed over for a promotion and I know that means the end of my rise within this company. I would like to leave immediately but the only position I've found open with another firm

pays no more than the job I have now. Should I take it anyway to save face?

No. Never make a lateral or downward move. Hold onto your current job until you can find one that pays more or offers better opportunity or both.

8.   I would like to move to another company which has made me a good offer but I've only been with my present firm a year and I'm afraid such a quick move would look bad on my resumé.

Take the offer. Don't worry about getting a reputation as a job hopper until you reach your middle thirties. That's about the average time to settle down with one firm.

9.   I'm almost forty-five and haven't reached executive level. I know authorities say I won't now because I'm too old but I think I can.

Good for you. If you can't get where you want with your present firm, you may do better in another, but look the situation over very carefully before changing jobs after forty.

10.   I've always wanted a dress shop of my own and now I have the opportunity to buy one. I'm very enthusiastic about it but my husband doesn't like the idea.

Before going into your own business, make sure you've thought through all the details. If you're prepared to spend less time with your family, and to deal with the nitty gritty duties of book-keeping, taxes, employee relations—all of which are totally your responsibility—proceed apace. If not, cool it.

11.   How much of my salary should I put into savings and investments?

A minimum of 10 percent.

Money Off the Job

Expanding What You Have

Don't think of the money you receive as stretching only from paycheck to paycheck. Instead imagine a succession of monthly or weekly or semi-weekly checks stretched over a whole year. Each check you receive is not an entity in itself. It's part of a whole, like a raindrop in the ocean. Now think of the years' checks stretching from now until you're sixty-five.

Did you know that money invested at 7 percent doubles itself in 10 years? If you start an investment program today, 10 years from now you will be very pleased with your foresight—and your investments.

Learn to think of money as accumulative. Learn to think of yourself as administering it, capably and efficiently without anxiety or stress.

Forget all those things you want to buy now, this minute, this month. Imagine yourself at sixty-five. What are you going to want to buy then? It's very hard when you're twenty-five to imagine yourself as thirty-five, let alone sixty-five. But believe me, when you're sixty-five, you're going to buy much the same things you buy now, food, shelter, clothing, entertainment, gifts. You'll still need to have your hair done and see your dentist.

With people living longer, sixty-five hardly rates as elderly anymore. I know several eighty-five-year-old women who maintain their own homes, drive their own cars, do most of their own housework, and keep up an active social life—living much as they did twenty years before.

But what are you going to live on when you're sixty-five? The steady paycheck may stop coming in. If you've spent every penny you earned all these years, how are you going to pay the bills then? Social Security? Social Security payments put you almost at the poverty level. Perhaps you're counting on a company pension. That can be skimpy too.

The Social Security Commission has revealed that 98 percent of all Americans are not financially ready to retire when their turn comes. To live reasonably well in your later years, you must start as soon as possible to build an estate.

BUILDING AN ESTATE

Most people have about 40 income-earning years. Let's say you earn $500 a month during those 40 years. Let's assume you never receive a raise, a bonus or anything else. How much will you have earned at the end of 40 years?

$$\$500 \times 12 \text{ (months)} = \$6,000.$$
$$\$6,000 \times 40 \text{ (years)} = \$240,000.$$

Almost a quarter of a million dollars.

You probably earn well over $500 a month so *it's quite likely that during your lifetime you will earn more than one million dollars. How much of it are you going to keep?*

I know living expenses are high. But if you try hard enough, you can hold onto some of that earned income and multiply it by investing it. When you no longer earn a paycheck, you can live in financial comfort because you still have money working for you. We'll go into where to put your money to work later. Now let's consider how much you need to put into investments.

Let's say your long-time financial goal is to have a $100,000 estate by the time you're sixty-five. The amount you need to set aside in order to achieve your goal depends obviously upon your age. If you're young, you can get a head start. If you're up in years, you're going to have to work harder at it but you can do it.

Age Twenty-five

That's a nice age to start on your ultimate $100,000. And it's easy to do, according to the textbooks. All you have to do is invest $1,075 where you're reasonably sure of 12 percent compounded interest, and ala kazam, when you're sixty-five, you'll have $100,000.

There are two big problems with these figures. First, most twenty-five-year-olds don't have $1,075 in a lump sum which they can use for investing. Second, 12 percent compounded interest isn't to be found at this writing and hasn't been for several years. Even 10 percent is hard to find.

You'll need to set aside $15 for investment, less than $4.00 a week. That sum properly invested will provide you more than $100,000 in forty years.

Age Thirty-five

If you invest $3,340 at 12 percent compounded, you'll reach the $100,000 in 30 years. Or settle for 10 percent compounded and put in a little more.

If you have no lump sum, you can invest $30 a month at 10 percent every month from now until you're sixty-five, and come out with the same end product. Consider this a bill which must be paid every month without exception. And if you can invest more, do so by all means.

Age Forty-five

You need a lump sum of approximately $10,500 to invest to reach your $100,000 goal. Or $100 a month for the next twenty years.

Age Fifty-five

Artur Rubinstein once told an interviewer who asked about his longevity that after fifty, it's patch, patch, patch. If you're fifty-five and haven't planned for age sixty-five, you have a lot of financial patching to do. But it's worth biting the bullet now in order to feel secure in ten years.

You need more than $32,000 in a lump sum to invest at 10 percent or about $450 each month for the next ten years.

Whatever your age, plan to enjoy life as long as you have it. Study the investment possibilities described in the following pages. Pick one, two, or even three of them and start your own investment program immediately.

You will understand the investment picture quicker if you remember the following principle: The safer the investment, the smaller the return. A few investments are in fact so safe that they cost you money.

SAVINGS ACCOUNTS

Financial advisers used to recommend that people keep an amount equal to five months' living expenses in their savings accounts. This is just a rule of thumb that's so general that it's almost useless. Everybody's needs are different and depend on different factors, such as:

- how much money you have in cash or checking accounts and can lay your hands on quickly
- your age
- your health
- your capabilities
- if you have dependents, their number and age

You will have to determine how much you want in your savings account but before you make a decision, understand fully the position of your savings account in the overall financial picture.

Disadvantages of Savings Accounts

Interest rates on savings accounts change from time to time but they've been 5¼ percent for quite a while. Banks and savings and loan societies advertise that they pay the maximum interest on your savings account, and they do. The interest rate is set by the federal government.

The rate of inflation also varies but let's say it's running 7 percent. Suppose you have $100 in a savings account.

At the End of One Year Because of Inflation

You will have lost	$7.00
You will have earned in compounded interest	$5.39
You will have lost on your money	$1.61

Also, interest on savings accounts is taxable so you will pay tax on that. Deduct another portion, the amount depending upon your income bracket.

Finally, you are losing the profit you could make if that $100 were in a more profitable investment.

Advantages of Savings Accounts

On the other hand, you have more money than you would have had if you'd simply spent the $100.

You also must consider the security aspect. A savings account provides peace of mind. You have cash to cover an emergency.

If You Must Have a Savings Account

Keep as little money in it as seems practicable to you.

If you have enough money from other sources to take care of emergencies, I advise you to avoid savings accounts. I have one client who is wealthy, but insists on keeping a sizeable savings account. She says, "Oh, it's so little trouble." And I say, "That's true, but you might be troubled if you knew how much you lost last year."

If you had put $10,000 in 1949 into a bank or savings and loan at a daily compounded 5¼ percent, in 1972 you would have had a total of $37,152.23.

If you put the $10,000 into reliable mutual funds at the same time, you would have been worth $103,898. These figures come from a good, conservative mutual fund.

If You Must Keep Money in a Savings Account

Make sure the institution compounds interest every day. You don't want straight interest; you want interest compounded daily. This means that interest is paid on your original lump sum, plus on the interest it has earned each day. If the regular interest is 5¼ percent, this daily compounding will result in an actual interest rate earned of about 5.39 percent. Although the law sets the interest rate, it does not specify compound or straight interest, so you have to shop.

There will also be differences in times you may withdraw your money and still get the maximum interest.

Ask several banks and savings and loans for their printed information on the various savings plans they offer, and study them well. They are in competition with each other for your dollars, so some will offer better terms than others.

Once your savings account builds to the proper size, you can go into another super-safe investment.

CERTIFICATES OF DEPOSIT

Commonly called CD's, these usually are available at banks and savings and loans. They normally come in amounts of $1,000, though you can find them for $500. CD's pay better than savings accounts because you are lending your money for a longer period. The higher interest may even be enough to take care of probable inflation.

You can buy CD's for periods of from three months to seven years. The short-term ones pay a smaller interest rate than the longer-term ones. In 1977 they ran from 5½ percent for short ones up to 7 percent and 7¾ percent for the longest available.

Plain CD's pay straight interest mostly quarterly, sometimes semi-annually. But look for compounded interest. On the short ones, 5½ percent, if compounded daily, works out to about 5.69 on an annual yield basis, and one with a base rate of 7¼ percent if compounded daily figures out to about a 7.72 percent annual return.

A good place to look for compounded interest is among big banks that can afford to attract your money with a daily compounding.

The interest rates available fluctuate rather gradually with conditions in the general money market, which has a convenient indicator called the *prime rate*. This is the amount big banks charge their very best and biggest customer companies. There is always much ado about it in newspapers whenever the big banks change it up or down.

You may cash in part or all of your CD's at any time whether or not they've reached maturity. If you cash in prior to maturity, you're charged a penalty, usually the interest on the amount withdrawn that it earned in the part of the calendar quarter-year in which you withdrew it. This is not a tremendous amount so you needn't worry about it.

When you're shopping for CD's, ask about time deposits because some banks invent their own names for Certificates of Deposit.

TREASURIES

Other very secure investments are Treasuries, bonds, notes, and bills. They are the direct obligation of the United States government. While our government changes as the voters decide, its obligations are always honored, which means Treasuries are very secure investments.

Institutions and big companies are the largest buyers of federal government securities, but about 20 percent of them are purchased by individuals. There are no specific figures on how many are owned by women or men, but it's safe to guess that women are about half of the individual owners.

Treasury Bonds are obligations that mature at face value in seven years or more, and come in minimum amounts of $1,000. They carry a fixed interest rate which is payable semi-annually to the holder. Probably the best known government bonds are the Series E and Series H bonds.

Series E bonds come in multiples of $25 in maturity value. They are sold at a discount from their face value so that, if held until they mature, they yield 6 percent. While they can be redeemed at any time after two months, their fixed redemption value at the time you redeem them results in less than the 6 percent return.

Series H bonds come in minimum denominations of $500 and are sold at face value. They pay interest semi-annually on a graduated scale which works out to 6 percent if held to maturity. They can be redeemed at par (face value) after six months from purchase date, but redemption prior to maturity results in less than the 6 percent interest.

Many people bought Series E bonds and still have them long after their original maturity date, but they still earn interest which you get when you finally redeem them. The interest to the time of redemption is taxable. However, you can exchange the Series E for Series H without having a tax liability at that time for the accumulated interest on the E's. But when the Series H bond is redeemed, all that interest is taxable. If you're old enough, you can plan to collect that interest when your personal exemptions rise along with your age.

Treasury Notes have maturities of from one to seven years, and the unit is also $1,000. Interest is handled the same way as bond interest.

Treasury Bills have a minimum face amount of $10,000 and are strictly short term, usually for 90 days, 182 days, and one year. However, the bills are sold at a discount from their par (face) value, and the difference between the amount paid for them and the face value at which they are paid off is your interest. Naturally their short term results in a lower rate of interest earned than on the bonds or notes, merely reflecting the current money market. I see little attraction in the bills for a private investor.

Advantages of Treasuries

One of the best things about Treasuries is their high degree of marketability. There is a tremendously active secondary market for them, so you can sell them quickly if necessary. They represent quick cash with interest up to date of sale.

Another good feature is their exemption from state and local taxes. This also insures a fast, uniform market for them throughout the country. If you live in a state or community which levies income or personal property taxes on your investments, they are worth considering.

How to Read Them

To train your eye how to read the daily reports of the markets on Treasuries, see the example and description following. When you consider that $\frac{1}{32}$ of a point is only 31¼ cents on a $1,000 bond, you realize how close these markets are.

How to Buy and Sell Treasuries

When Treasury bonds, notes, and bills are first offered, they're sold through the Federal Reserve banks. If you buy them there, you pay no commission. If you go through a commercial bank or the average securities dealer, you're faced with a probable $25 minimum commission. That's 2½ points on one $1,000 bond, ¼ point on $10,000. There goes a good slice of your interest yield.

If you want to sell Treasuries, you go to some of the largest national brokerage houses, who likely have offices near you. These firms have gone into actively trading Treasuries for their own account and deal with the Fed. They will very likely make you a "net" bid—no commission because they'll buy from you for their trading account.

The securities are usually sold at weekly auctions held through the Federal Reserve banks, and announced in advance. You can go to or phone the nearest Federal Reserve bank or branch and get full information on how to participate in the auction, although you do not personally attend. It is important to tell officials at the bank that you are a private investor and want to bid non-competitively.

They will want a good faith deposit before the sale to insure that you are serious and will follow through. On the day of the sale, the big institutional buyers submit their bids, and the securities are sold at the least interest cost to the Treasury. There will be a range of prices they will accept to sell the whole issue to the competitive bidders and still have some for the private sector. Your price will be the average of the competitive bids they accept.

The bids received by all the Fed banks and their branches are fed into a central computer to see who gets how many at what price, and to figure the average price—the one that is important to you. The re-

EXAMPLE OF DAILY QUOTATIONS ON TREASURY BONDS AND NOTES

Treasury bonds and notes

NEW YORK (AP) — Closing Over-the-Counter U.S. Treasury Bonds for Tuesday.

Rate	Mat.	date	Bid	Asked	Bid Chg	Yld
8.38	Sep	1977 n	100	100.2	.....	0.26
7.50	Oct	1977 n	100.1	100.3	.....	6.22
7.75	Nov	1977 n	100.4	100.6	.....	6.09
6.63	Nov	1977 n	100	100.2	.....	6.12
7.25	Dec	1977 n	100.5	100.7	.....	6.26
6.38	Jan	1978 n	99.31	100.1	.....	6.22
6.25	Feb	1978 n	99.29	99.31	.....	6.29
8.00	Feb	1978 n	100.19	100.23	.....	6.20
6.75	Mar	1978 n	100.4	100.6	.....	6.36
6.50	Apr	1978 n	99.31	100.3	.....	6.33
7.13	May	1978 n	100.11	100.15	.....	6.35
7.88	May	1978 n	100.25	100.29	.....	6.38
7.13	May	1978 n	100.13	100.17+	.2	6.30
6.88	Jun	1978 n	100.7	100.11+	.2	6.40
6.88	Jul	1978 n	100.7	100.11+	.1	6.45
7.63	Aug	1978 n	100.27	100.31+	.1	6.47
8.75	Aug	1978 n	101.25	101.29	.....	6.48
6.63	Aug	1978 n	100	100.4 +	.2	6.48
6.25	Sep	1978 n	99.20	99.24+	.2	6.51
5.88	Oct	1978 n	99.6	99.10+	.1	6.54
6.00	Nov	1978 n	99.10	99.14+	.1	6.52
5.75	Nov	1978 n	99	99.4 +	.2	6.54
5.25	Dec	1978 n	98.10	98.14+	.2	6.57
8.13	Dec	1978 n	101.24	101.28+	.3	6.55
5.88	Jan	1979 n	98.31	99.3 +	.1	6.60
7.00	Feb	1979 n	100.13	100.17+	.2	6.59
5.88	Feb	1979 n	98.26	98.30....	..	6.60
6.00	Mar	1979 n	99.2	99.6 +	.2	6.58
5.88	Apr	1979 n	98.26	98.30+	.2	6.59
6.13	May	1979 n	99.4	99.6 +	.2	6.65
7.88	May	1979 n	101.25	101.29+	.3	6.62
6.13	Jun	1979 n	99.3	99.5 +	.3	6.64
7.75	Jun	1979 n	101.22	101.26+	.3	6.64
6.25	Jul	1979 n	99.6	99.8 +	.4	6.69
6.25	Aug	1979 n	99.4	99.8 +	.3	6.69
6.63	Aug	1979 n	99.23	99.25+	.5	6.75
6.88	Aug	1979 n	100.4	100.8 +	.4	6.73
6.63	Sep	1979 n	99.23	99.25+	.6	6.75
6.50	Sep	1979 n	103.4	103.8 +	.2	6.74
6.25	Nov	1979 n	98.28	99 +	.3	6.76
6.63	Nov	1979 n	99.20	99.24+	.4	6.75
7.00	Nov	1979 n	100.10	100.14+	.4	6.78
7.50	Dec	1979 n	101.10	101.14+	.4	6.80
4.00	Feb	1980 n	94.6	94.22	....	6.44
6.50	Feb	1980 n	99.7	99.11+	.5	6.80
7.60	Mar	1980 n	101.1	101.19+	.4	6.79
6.88	May	1980 n	100.1	100.9 +	.4	6.76
7.63	Jun	1980 n	101.26	102.2 +	.3	6.76
6.75	Aug	1980 n	99.20	99.24+	.6	6.85
9.00	Aug	1980 n	105.14	105.22+	.3	6.80
6.88	Sep	1980 n	99.28	100.4 +	.3	6.83
3.50	Nov	1980 n	91.26	92.10.....		6.24
5.88	Dec	1980 n	97.2	97.10+	.4	6.81
7.00	Feb	1981 n	100.8	100.16+	.6	6.83
7.38	Feb	1981 n	101.8	101.16+	.5	6.87
6.88	Mar	1981 n	99.23	99.31+	.6	6.89
7.38	May	1981 n	101.9	101.17+	.5	6.89
6.75	Jun	1981 n	99.9	99.13+	.6	6.93
7.00	Aug	1981	100.6	100.22+	.2	6.79
7.63	Aug	1981 n	102.4	102.12+	.6	6.91
6.75	Sep	1981 n	99.6	99.8 +	.5	6.97
7.00	Nov	1981 n	99.30	100.6 +	.4	6.95
7.75	Nov	1981 n	102.9	102.27-	.5	6.94
6.13	Feb	1982 n	96.20	96.28+	.7	6.97
6.38	Feb	1982	97.10	97.26+	.4	6.96
7.00	May	1982 n	99.29	100.1 +	.9	6.99
8.00	May	1982 n	103.22	103.30+	.6	6.99
8.13	Aug	1982 n	104.7	104.16+	.7	7.03
7.88	Nov	1982 n	103.11	103.19+	.8	7.02
8.00	Feb	1983 n	103.30	104.6 +	.8	7.05
3.25	Jun	1978-83	83.18	84.18+	.4	6.53
7.00	Nov	1983 n	99.20	99.28+	.9	7.02
7.25	Feb	1984 n	100.8	100.12+	.9	7.18
6.38	Aug	1984	95.10	96.10-	.6	7.06
7.25	Aug	1984 n	100.5	100.9 +	.8	7.20
3.25	May	1985	79.28	80.20.....		6.47
4.25	May	1975-85	83.26	84.26....		6.84
7.88	May	1986 n	103.10	103.18+	.9	7.31
8.00	Aug	1986 n	104.8	104.12+	.8	7.32
6.13	Nov	1986	93.14	94 14...	.9	6.96
3.50	Feb	1990	78.8	79.8 -	.2	5.88
8.25	May	1990	106.12	106.28+	.5	7.40
4.25	Aug	1987-92	79.12	80.12...	.	8.30
2.25	Aug	1992	98.1	98.5 +	.6	7.45
4.00	Feb	1988-93	78.30	79.30....		6.02
6.75	Feb	1993	95.16	96.16-	.4	7.13
7.50	Aug	1988-93	100.22	101.22+	.2	7.27
4.13	May	1989-94	78.18	79.18...	.	6.10
3.00	Feb	1995	78.6	79.6		4.78
7.00	May	1993-98	96.4	97.4 +	.2	7.26
3.50	Nov	1998	78.14	79.14+	.2	5.10
8.50	May	1994-99	107.20	108.4 +	.1	7.63
7.88	Feb	1995-00	102.6	102.14+	.2	7.62
8.38	Aug	1995-00	106.20	107.4 +	.3	7.63
8.00	Aug	1996-01	103.6	103.14+	.2	7.65
8.25	May	2000-05	105.26	106.10+	.6	7.66
7.63	Feb	2002-07	99.12	99.20+	.6	7.66

n— Treasury notes.

Bid and asked prices quoted in dollars and thirty seconds. Subject to Federal taxes but not to State income taxes.

Column by column, the information shown is:

1. The security's interest rate
2. Its month of maturity
3. Its year of maturity

(if followed by n, this is a note; if none, this is a bond)

4. The price bid for them
5. The price at which they're offered
6. The change in bid price since yesterday
7. Their yield to maturity at this price.

The unit of price change in quotations on Treasuries is $\frac{1}{32}$ of a point, a point being 1 percent of the face value. Other bonds and stocks are quoted with a unit change of $\frac{1}{8}$ of a point.

sults are announced in the next day's news. At this time, if you have made a purchase, be sure you pay the balance and carry out your contract on the day the bonds are ready for delivery, which you'll be told.

Both the announcements of sales and results are broadcast to the press, but only newspapers with good financial sections or the *Wall Street Journal* publish them.

If you don't live near a Federal Reserve bank or branch, you can write the one nearest you for information on what procedure to follow to buy Treasuries. You should do this well in advance of when you want to enter an order so you'll be prepared when an issue comes along that you think you'd like to buy into. Your library, bank, or Chamber of Commerce can provide you with the address of the nearest Federal Reserve bank.

OTHER FEDERAL BONDS

While Treasury securities are direct obligations of the federal government, there are a number of federal agencies that issue bonds. These include the Federal Land Bank, Federal Home Loan Bank, Federal National Mortgage Association (Fannie Mae), Government National Mortgage Association (Ginnie Mae).

There are many maturities and a fairly active trading market on all of these. As usual the yields to maturity are higher in the longer ones.

If you're interested, there are so many of these bonds that you should look them up in technical books available in most libraries. One kind of bond is the *Ginnie Mae,* a strange, hybrid security with a combination of interest and pay-back of principal.

In 1970 when home mortgages were hard to obtain and then only at extremely high interest rates, Congress formed the Government National Mortgage Association to aid both the building industry and the many people needing to build homes. It is a pool of many single-family mortgages, and the pool is backed by the GNMA and Federal Housing Administration (or Veterans' Administration). Investors can buy certificates in the pool without worry about their investment, and get their money in the form of interest and principal repayments without the trouble of collections, possible foreclosures, or the like. That work is all done for them, hence the certificates are known as "pass-throughs."

The pool receives payments on homeowners' mortgages which include both interest and a payment on the principal. As you receive your payments from the pool, part of it is interest and that is taxable. But as the mortgages in the pool are either paid off or refinanced, you get your share of the repaid principal too. Since it's part of your money coming back, it's not taxable.

Experience has shown that on the average, home mortgages get paid off in about twelve years. If every mortgage in the pool just paid the monthly interest and principal, each check you get would be just so much on interest and the rest on principal. But each time a mortgage is refinanced, or prepaid by the homeowner, there is that much principal to be distributed in advance as an "extra" to the certificate holders. This, and the regular installments on principal, are not taxable. Just your proportional share of the pool's interest receipts.

Originally, the lowest amount you could buy from a broker was $100,000. But now several large brokerage firms may buy a million or more dollars' worth, and offer certificates of participation as small as $10,000. These can be very interesting to retirees, or those planning to retire soon, for three reasons: First, they are safe. Second, they offer high return. Third, your personal responsibilities once you've made the purchase are minimal. Of course when you've received back all the money you invested as principal, you've had your money back and that's the end. But as your principal receipts or "extras" get substantial, you can reinvest them, possibly in stocks.

So far, I've stuck to conservative ways for you to put your money to work efficiently and safely. Now it's time to hunt for more profitable investments. The logical place is where you can become a partner instead of merely a lender. That means stocks.

STOCK MARKET

Some think of the stock market as a dangerous jungle, and they're partly right. But investing in stocks of sturdy, growing businesses is a way you can increase your total dollars to keep up with or even ahead of inflation's erosion. The younger you are, the more this can help you build your financial worth.

Before you ever get into the market, you should do three things:

- determine your goals
- study the market itself so you know how it works and what to expect of it
- study investment possibilities of companies in whose stock you may want to invest

"The cardinal rule of investing is to set your objective," says Mary Wren, a vice president of the largest investment and brokerage firm in the United States, Merrill Lynch, Pierce, Fenner & Smith. You may want to change your goal later but in the meantime it's a beacon to head for. Perhaps you want to build an independent income, pay for a vacation home, take a world cruise. Whatever you want, get into the *habit* of working toward the goal instead of letting your life and your money flow past you.

What Is the Stock Market?

The stock market is actually a vast array of markets for bonds and stocks. The name is an easy way to include the New York Stock Exchange, the American Stock Exchange, other exchanges in principal cities, and the so-called Over The Counter Market, whose countless securities don't happen to be listed on an exchange but are traded among brokers over the phone in varying degrees of activity.

Stocks can be divided into two primary kinds, growth and income.

Growth Stocks

A young client of mine says her husband complains that the *Wall Street Journal* has replaced him in bed. This twenty-five-year-old is determined to have a million dollars before she's thirty-five, starting from scratch. Having set her sights high over a short 10 years, she is inclined toward growth stocks. Fortunately she is an adventurous soul with steady nerves.

A growth company is most often one in the newer technical fields, and tends to plow back a large share of its earnings into research and development rather than pay fat dividends. A substantial part of their market price represents prospects for the future rather than past performance. So, growth stocks can make money for you now instead of over 10 or 20 years of good dividend income. Also, they are quite risky and can give you a ride like a roller-coaster.

Typical are the companies in the electronics and computer fields, although some of these have reached a stature and conservatism that are enviable. Even the latter can dizzy you with their ups and downs as their competitors bloom or fade. They take an extra amount of watching if you buy them.

Income Stocks

The market on income stocks moves far less spectacularly than on growth stocks, but you get a better average dividend income. And you sleep better.

Typical of the income stocks are those of the larger utility companies. As population grows, so does their business, and they particularly like to have as many of their customers as possible as stockholders. Utilities are regulated and stockholders are voters who will show their displeasure if the politicians don't allow the company to earn a fair profit on its total investment and above its operating expenses. A good dividend rate will attract customers to become stockholders.

Many investors try to include both income and growth stocks in their portfolio (their total holdings). With both types represented, you have income from the market as well as an investment in the future.

Never invest funds in the market that you may need soon.

Don't think of the money you put there as being readily available to you, even though you can sell your stocks very easily. The trouble is if you're forced to sell, stocks may be down and you will have to take a loss. You also interrupt long-term investing plans. When you invest in the market, do it with funds you don't expect to need for some years.

I Want to Emphasize the Importance of Long-Term Planning and Investing in the Stock Market.

In the history of our country, rising national prosperity has been the pattern, with a setback from time to time. The market has always risen and dropped, gone higher and dipped again. Keep yourself in a financial position to wait out the dips and you'll probably make money.

Guides in the Stock Market Jungle

Many guides are available to you and you should take advantage of them before getting into the market. They include:

* Reading material
* Literature prepared by large companies
* *Wall Street Week*, a weekly half hour TV show on Public Broadcasting
* A good broker
* Observation of products when you're shopping
* Exchange of information with friends and acquaintances
* Trade publications

Your first guide should be *reading material*.

Newspapers: To be sure you get all the news of the corporate world, read the *Wall Street Journal*. It's excellent. So is *The New York Times*, daily and Sunday. Your favorite daily newspaper may also have a good financial section. *Barron's* National Business and Financial Weekly is useful. Financial news will keep you informed on general business conditions and the basic movements of the money market.

Standard and Poor's Stock Guide is a good reference. Your local library probably has it, or write to Standard & Poor's Corporation, 345 Hudson Street, New York, New York 10014, for a list of their services. Use it as a first reference to check on a company that comes to your mind after reading a news item or from conversation.

TV: I strongly recommend "Wall Street Week," a TV show on the Public Broadcasting System. Check your local listings for the time it's shown in your area. Panelists are experienced investment personalities who know how to stay non-technical enough for lay viewers.

Company literature: Write for the annual statement if you're interested in a company. They'll give you some idea of how the company is doing, and whether you might want to invest in it. The makers of many products you may be familiar with are no longer independent, but are divisions of a much larger conglomerate. Amana kitchen equipment, for instance, comes from a division of Raytheon Corporation; the famous Pratt & Whitney aircraft engines are a part of United Technologies; the Burger King chain belongs to Pillsbury.

Observe while shopping: You'll be surprised how much you can learn while doing your shopping. Are some demands increasing and others slacking off? Who makes what? Even at social gatherings I find women avidly trading useful news about new products or shopping centers.

Trade publications: Technical progress of all kinds is often reported first in trade publications. If you work for a company that subscribes to any of these, read them and be alert for anything new or better described in articles or advertisements. Such information is often there long before it makes a splash in mass media headlines.

FINDING A BROKER

You find a good broker in much the same manner as you select a doctor, a dentist, or attorney. Talk to friends and relatives. When someone recommends a broker, give him a call and see how you like him. Talk with several until you find one with a good track record who is compatible with you, and with a well known, reputable firm.

Your broker should be familiar with the trading of stocks and bonds listed on the major exchanges, and can supply you with a lot of information that the firm's analysts dig up. Your brokerage firm doubtless will have specialists in government securities, commodities, and other areas, to whom your broker can turn for advice if necessary.

The broker of your choice will have to ask you certain questions and fill out a form required by the Securities and Exchange Commission (SEC). The form shows all possible questions to be answered for any type of account, many of which will not apply to you. Your broker will know what answers he needs.

Doing Business With a Broker

After the agreement is completed and signed, you will do most of your business by phone. You will pay a commission each time you buy or sell. Ask the broker for a way to figure what this will be. It varies with the price of the stock and the number of shares (or bonds) involved.

The commission is surprisingly modest when you consider charges in other professions, yet I know people who will stay out of the market because they object to paying it. A simple order to buy stock involves much communication and bookkeeping. The broker certainly earns his fee.

After each transaction you will receive a confirmation in the mail showing all the details, including whether the firm bought or sold something on the market *for* you (plus or minus commission) or whether they sold *to* you or bought *from* you (acting for themselves, with no commission).

Be sure you keep these confirmations in a safe place. You will need them to support your profit or loss statement on your income-tax return. More on this later.

You must pay for your purchases by the fifth business day following the actual purchase. Conversely, you will be sent a check for your money within five working days.

If at some time your broker offers you a bond or stock at a "net" price, with no commission, it most likely is part of a new issue just being publicly offered. His firm has joined the syndicate or banking group that has underwritten the entire issue, and the group's selling commission is being paid by the issuing company, which is getting the money.

Sometimes, also, a brokerage house maintains a market for a bond or stock that is not listed on an exchange. Then, they will buy it or sell it, acting as "principal." It's likely to be some issue their analysts think is selling too cheaply. The firm's trading department is then authorized to become active in buying and selling it for their own account. At the same time while they have their own money backing their judgment, they will offer it to their customers as a favor.

Where to Keep Your Stocks

In my opinion the best place for your stocks, especially growth stocks, is in your account with your broker. That way it takes only a phone call to get out or in, which makes it convenient whether you're at home, on vacation, or in Keokuk, Iowa, for a family wedding. The brokerage firm receives your dividends first and sends you a check. It will all show on your monthly statement so you'll have it at income-tax time.

HOW TO JUDGE A POTENTIAL INVESTMENT

Start your study of some large, well-established businesses that do something, or make something, that most everybody needs or wants. Find out how long they've been in business, and how their profits and dividends have been over the years. Then, dig a little deeper and see how much money they owe. Do you think it's bad if a company has a large debt? It depends on what business they're in, as you will see. Some of the debt will be their day-to-day bank loans, which mostly are to smooth the flow between paying their bills and getting paid by their customers. They probably pay the "prime rate" of interest, which is the lowest rate the banks charge their best customers. There probably will be bonds, secured by mortgages on some or all of their properties; also "debentures" or "notes," which are really only promises to pay, although they may have certain assets or earnings pledged to that end. The interest rates all these pay depend on the money market that existed when the issues were sold.

Bear this in mind about a company's debt. No managers in their right mind borrow money unless they feel certain that they can earn far more on that money than what they are paying for it. So in most cases, it pays a large, well-run company to borrow what they can at reasonable rates.

Preferred and Common Stock

The earnings of a company after interest and taxes are what is available to stockholders. These stocks come in the form of preferred and common stock. Technically they both represent ownership or what's called "equity investment." The preferred stock is entitled to its fixed dividends before the common stock gets paid. But that's *all* it's entitled to, no matter how much the firm makes. So the real owners are the holders of the common stock.

If you are willing to assume the risk of being an owner instead of a lender in a company, you are better off with the common. Inflation, plus improved earnings through good management, will likely see higher earnings, higher dividends, and a higher price for common stock. That means that you would be gaining in numbers of dollars to offset the erosion in purchasing power of each one. You would be doing something to protect yourself against inflation. In the meantime, the prices of the debt issues and the preferred stocks will move up or down only as a reflection of the current bank interest rates, usually within relatively narrow limits.

P/E Ratio

You are most interested in how much a company is earning, after all expenses and taxes, on each share of common stock. The relation between the stock's price and its earnings is the price-earnings or P/E ratio.

A stock selling at 30 and earning $5.00 annually has a price-earnings ratio of 30/5 or a P/E of 6. If the price goes to 40 and the earnings are still $5.00, the ratio becomes 40/5: a P/E of 8. The lower P/E is the more attractive.

The amount of dividend the stock pays has nothing whatever to do with its P/E ratio. The dividend determines only your current *yield*. In the above case, assume the stock pays an annual dividend of $2.50. If you pay 30 for it, your yield is 2.50/30 or 8.33 percent. If you buy it at 40, the yield is 2.50/40 which is 6.25 percent.

But don't lose sight of what you are trying to do, which is to beat the probable rate of inflation. Your decision to buy is based mainly on your own confidence, after study, that the company will continue not only to do as well as it has, but also that it will do better.

If possible, leave your dividends in your investment account to add to your next purchase so they too will be working for you.

Suppose you have been studying a company you know is solid and well managed, and you find that the P/E ratio is about 6 or 7. You see other companies you know by reputation in similar lines of business, whose stocks have a P/E of 8, 9, or 10. Maybe these others have something that doesn't meet the eye or have done something to reduce their costs or improve their sales. But the reason may be much simpler. Maybe fewer people have studied the company you're interested in. They may be studying it now, however, and wonder why a company as good as that is selling at a P/E of only 6 instead of 9. A lot of smart people are looking for bargains, just as you are. They range from professional analysts to small but careful investors. Sooner or later when enough of them decide the stock is too cheap, the incoming orders will move it up, so don't wait too long deciding whether or not to buy. If you're fairly certain of your facts, buy before the price goes up.

Set Your Top Price

When you decide to buy a stock at a certain P/E ratio, you should also decide how much it should increase. Plan when you buy at what price you think you want to cash in. If the price moves up close to that, study it again. Maybe it really is time to sell, or perhaps the company's business and profits have increased so much that you want to reset your sights to a higher price. Let that decision be based on just as critical a look as you gave it before you bought.

Two Important Don'ts

1) Don't buy and sell every time a stock moves a couple of points. You will only enrich your broker instead of yourself.

2) Don't make the mistake of thinking you must buy at the very bottom and sell at the very top. If market fluctuations make you so nervous you forget the goal you set, you don't belong in the stock market.

After the First Purchase

Continue to ferret out other situations you may want to invest in. At the same time keep a watch on your company. Compare it to the general market. Watch for news releases and quarterly earnings statements from your company.

When To Sell

Don't become sentimental about your stocks. If one doesn't perform well, weed it out. If you see one of your companies dragging its feet when others in the field are prospering, part company. You can deduct the loss on your tax return. It's the *average* performance of your choices that counts. No one wins 'em all, not even the sharpest financiers.

Stocks and Taxes

When you sell, show on your tax return what you received after all charges have been deducted.

If you decide to sell near the end of the tax year, take any losses to reduce your tax. Bear in mind that the day you sell must leave at least five working days in that tax year for the actual stock to be delivered to the *buyer*—not to your broker. If your broker isn't keeping all your stocks, be sure he has the proper one in plenty of time to deliver to the buyer's broker before the tax year is gone.

Under the Tax Reform Act of 1976, the length of time you have to hold an investment to qualify it as a long-term gain is a full year plus one day.

Can You Trust Your Hunches?

As you become familiar with business news and the market, you will from time to time experience what may seem to be intuitive hunches to buy or sell some particular stock. Actually these thoughts don't just come to you out of thin air. Your mind is the most marvelous computer in the world. It has absorbed information and coordinated apparently unrelated news items. It may suddenly fit bits and pieces together that were stored in the memory bank and presto! you get a hunch to act. If you hadn't been reading, studying, and observing trends, those bits and pieces of information wouldn't have been there for your mental computer to put together. I believe most so-called intuition is really a product of experience and observation.

Warnings

The stock market is no place to get rich in a hurry. Don't base your investing on tips from uninformed persons. Stick to reliable sources of information and advice from your broker.

MUTUAL FUNDS

If you haven't the time to study and pick your own investments but still like the idea of being in the stock market, you may be interested in mutual funds.

Mutual funds are formed by companies whose entire function is to do the work of analysis, market watching, and buying and selling for the pooled funds. Officials of such companies are professionals.

Usually a mutual fund company manages a number of pools with different types of investments in each—from highly conservative, with their money largely in high-rated bonds, to what are called "growth" funds that specialize in the volatile issues with the purpose of increase in market value. In between are the "income" funds that, as the name implies, concentrate on stocks of sound companies which are paying good or better than average dividends. There are funds geared to any criteria of security, income or growth, so you can spread your investment among several, if you choose. Shares in mutual funds are quoted daily in most major newspapers.

Stock in the funds themselves is sold by a prospectus required to give all details and through sales personnel who are required to be licensed. The market value of the fund stocks is determined by averaging the price of all the stocks or bonds held by the fund. There is a "bid side" which is the liquidating value of the price of the fund's holdings in each investment. This is the price you get if you want to cash in your fund shares. The "asked side" is the price at which you can buy shares, which includes the commission.

One advantage of mutual funds is that through the pooling of many investors' money the managers are able to buy some of the high-priced blue-chip stocks that are too expensive for the average investor.

Regular Investments

Some years ago I attended a few mutual fund seminars and was impressed by the stress put on making a regular monthly investment. Until that time I had invested haphazardly whenever I had a little extra money. This was a commitment to a *plan* and that made sense to me.

I picked two funds, a fairly conservative one and one in the growth class. Both companies had good records. Sorry to say I never made a dime on either. They got off to a fast start and then went to sleep somewhere along the way.

However I did profit from the habit of setting aside a particular sum each month for investment. I learned not only the value of systematic investment but that this is the way you get a true dollar-cost average. By putting the same amount in the same fund on the same day each month, you can figure how much you have spent and how much you have profited in spite of the market's fluctuations.

If You're Interested in Mutuals

Investigate a number. The official prospectus and their latest financial statement show what securities are included in their portfolios, their cost, and their market values. This information gives you a broad picture of each fund's investment philosophy.

Attractive to Older Persons

Older people may find mutual fund shares attractive for two reasons.

1) Stock may be included in your estate. It's next to impossible to sell stocks until a will has been probated and there's the chance that while a will is in probate a certain stock that is behaving badly should be dumped without delay, but cannot be under the circumstances. But if the stock part of the estate were in mutual funds, the paid analysts who buy and sell for the fund can continue to act in the best interests of the portfolio and sell if necessary.

2) If a will has numerous bequests, the testator may want to leave certain percentages of his estate to his beneficiaries. Unless all the stock holdings are sold and the recipients get cash, it's almost impossible to split up various stocks selling at different prices so that all the heirs get exactly what the will indicates. If it's in a mutual fund, it can be accurately distributed to the third decimal in whatever proportion the testator said in his will.

BONDS

You should also know something about investing in bonds. It really isn't very different from buying stocks, except that you are buying a company's debt instead of becoming a company owner. Most bonds come in $1,000 face value denomination, known as par 100. Some also come in $500 face value, but they are harder to buy and sell. So the unit of trading is one bond of $1,000 face value.

Both Moody's Investment Service and Standard & Poor give ratings to bonds. They vary from AAA for top quality on down through B's and C. The ratings are based on the issuing company's apparent ability to promptly pay principal and interest and may be changed if the condition of the issuer changes. But they are a good quick guide to a company's general stature in the financial community. Bonds with the highest ratings command the highest market prices and consequent lower yields.

How to Read the Bond Market Reports

The daily trading in bonds listed on the New York Stock Exchange is shown by most large newspapers, but not all. They appear alphabetically by name of the company, and where there is more than one issue they are in the order of their maturity year, earliest first. Here are two of the American Telephone & Telegraph Company issues as they appeared recently.

Col.	(1)	(2)	(3)	(4)	(5)	(6)
ATT	2¾ s 80	221	92½	91¾	92⅛	+⅛
ATT	3⅞ s 90	119	71⅞	70½	71⅞	+⅞

Column (1) is the bond and its interest rate and maturity.
Column (2) is the number of bonds ($1,000) traded that day.
Columns (3) through (5) are the high, low, and last prices.
Column (6) is the change, up or down, from the closing the day before.

A big company like AT&T will have numerous bond issues, and now they run from interest rates of 2⅝ up to 8.80 percent. They mature at par (100) from 1979 to 2005. The company needs large amounts of money all the time for expansion and improvements, and the various rates and maturities result from the conditions in the money market at the time the issues were sold. In the early part of 1977 the interest rates on the average ran from 7 to 9 percent, depending on the credit rating of the company offering a new bond issue for sale.

So you'll find the low-interest, old bonds selling at a discount. The longer the maturity, the greater the discount. You have the same situation as when you invest in Treasuries or in CD's: the shorter term they are, the less interest you get on your investment. On a certain day, an example would be AT&T 2¾'s, due 1980, selling at 91, while their 3⅞'s due 1990, sold at 70⅜.

If you bought the 2¾'s at 91, the current yield on your money would be about 3 percent. (You divide the interest rate by the price.) If you hold them until they are paid off in two years at 100 in 1980, you'd have a profit of 9 points, or $90.00 on your principal, or about $45.00 per year. Added to your *current* yield of about 3 percent, your actual yield to maturity is about 7½ percent.

Now look what happens if you bought the 3⅞'s at 70⅞.

They don't mature until 1990, 12 years. The *current* yield is about 5½ percent. Over 12 years, if you keep them, you'd have a profit of about 29 points, or $290.00 per bond. This is about $24.17 per year that you hold them, and brings your yield to maturity to around 7.93 percent. It's the longer maturity that makes the difference. The long-term ones will, of course, move up or down more as a reflection of the money market.

The difference between your cost and the pay-off at 100 when they mature is a capital or long-term gain, and at this writing is taxed at a lesser rate than current income.

You will notice that high-grade bonds carrying interest rates up to 8¾ percent sell at well above their par value. Think about them differently. Bond issues are "callable" for pay-off by the company at various prices in different years of their life. You must determine what these call prices are and when each is effective. Bear in mind that if general interest rates drop enough, it pays the company to sell a new issue and redeem the old, high-interest ones. So while your current interest yield may be high, you must figure on a possible redemption sooner than you expected. If you paid over the call price, that loss has to be deducted from your interest income to see what the bonds would actually return you as a net yield.

Convertible Bonds

You may find a "cv" after a bond description. That means that this one is convertible into something—usually common stock—at the option of the holder, at certain prices for the common, and during certain periods. Such issues usually were originally sold when money was tight, and the company "sweetened" it to make it attractive to investors. These offer a possibility of profit from the conversion feature while still bearing a fixed interest rate and date of maturity as an obligation of the company. But be sure you know how long the conversion features last and at what prices, and watch them like a hawk so your conversion feature doesn't expire while you're thinking about something else.

GOING IT ALONE VS. INVESTMENT CLUBS

If you can't see yourself as a lone investor, one of the best ways to trade ideas is through membership in an investment club. These clubs usually start with a group of friends, neighbors, or co-workers interested in investments, who decide to pool their information, research, and funds for the benefit of all concerned.

If you're interested in starting a club of your own, write the National Association of Investment Clubs at P.O. Box 220, Royal Oak, Michigan 58068. Tell them your situation, ask for whatever they can send immediately along with a list of their publications and activities. Their manual, which sells for $3.00, will give you a complete description of starting a club and details of running it properly. For best results 15 members is a good size for a club and contributions to the "pool" should be made monthly in whatever base amount may be decided by members.

Club Adviser

One point you'll note if you send for the NAIC information is that no member of a club should be a broker. A good broker wants only to supply you with information on companies that his firm's analysts regularly provide. After he's done that, the club members make their own study of the stock, using procedures developed by NAIC. Your club broker will probably serve you as adviser for one year.

In my opinion, even if you intend to invest independently, membership in an investment club can be of great benefit through meetings with others, developing ideas, and pooling research. If you can't find an existing club, start one. You'll learn, it's stimulating, fun, and, if everything goes well, profitable.

COLLECTIONS AS AN INVESTMENT

Stamps and coins. They are probably collected more than any other item. Are they really an investment? They can be, but like everything else, require study. Their "values" are shown in catalogs which give an estimate of what a stamp or coin *should* bring to a dealer offering it for sale. If you use catalog prices to trade with a fellow collector, fine. Both parties are using the same yardstick. If you want to sell for cash, it's a different matter. Some real rarities may be snapped up well above the listed prices, while some items in plentiful supply may be almost impossible to move at any price. If you want to collect stamps or coins, join a philatelic or numismatic club and do a lot of listening to experienced members before thinking seriously about considering your hobby an investment.

Antiques. One area of collecting where, with care and study, you may profit is on antique furniture. However, successful investing in antiques takes even more study and experience than the stock market does. You must know the difference between the real thing and reproductions of little value. Authoritative books on furniture, glass, china, clocks, etc., are endless and require a great deal of study time. If you have a strong urge in this direction, I suggest starting with furniture because there will be more potential buyers for it than for antique china or glass, and that's important if you ever want to sell.

Paintings. Art as an investment is risky also unless you're buying masterpieces. If you know art, you may be able to pick a winner among unknown artists, but don't rely on the word of a gallery owner that a painting is a good investment because the artist will be famous *someday*. Better to buy one by an artist who is already widely acclaimed in the art world, even if you only buy one of his or her signed prints. These are usually offered in limited editions of so many numbered, signed copies. Even if a painting or print goes up in value, it's hard to find buyers. So buy art you enjoy; that may be all you get out of it.

Gems. Investing in gems is strictly for professionals. If you've ever tried to sell jewels you know you can get only a fraction of their worth. Better enjoy them on the hobby level.

REAL ESTATE

The highest yield you can get on an investment in the United States is in real estate. The national average of money made on real estate investments during the past years was 18 percent. In booming cities like Houston and New Orleans, it's 23 percent a year. Everyone who became wealthy in this country did it in real estate. Even though Andrew Carnegie was in steel and John D. Rockefeller in a variety of things, when they earned money, they built their fortunes by investing in real estate. Managed with care, it's the safest investment in the world. There are two billion useable acres of land in this country. In 1900 there were 76 million people who used this land. There are more than 200 million using the same land now. Do you see any indication that fewer people will be using it? The law of supply and demand says nothing will be more valuable than land and that which is put upon land.

Think about some community with which you're familiar. Think of some particular area which you considered a Godforsaken spot. Did you watch that area become the most valuable in town? I've done it. I've always excused myself by saying I was a little investor and there was nothing I could do about that land. The fact is I just lacked the foresight to do anything about it. But it's not too late for me—or for you. What has been done can be done again. Little investors can become big investors.

Advantages of Real Estate Investing

The advantages of investing in real estate are threefold.

1) It has a high return. When you can get 16 percent to 23 percent annual return on your money, it's great.

2) The tax picture is good if you invest in real estate, not raw land but land with buildings on it.

3)   Real estate has leverage. Leverage is the ability to own for all practical purposes a piece of property which you have not completely paid for. You can even resell it without ever first paying for it completely. Used sensibly, leverage is extremely profitable.

For example, I bought a lot for $3,000. I made a down payment of $1,000. I agreed to pay off the balance over five years. Before the first annual payment was due, I sold the lot for $4,000. What was my percentage of profit? In other words, how much interest did I make on the money?

The answer is *one hundred* percent. I spent, actually handed over, $1,000. I sold the property for $4,000. I paid off the loan and had $1,000 left. That was my profit. So I made 100 percent interest. It's hard to do better than that.

That's simplified, of course, because taxes, the cost of the sale, and other costs reduce the profit. But those were relatively minor expenses and the interest rate of the transaction was close to 100 percent.

Keep Down Payments Small

If I could have made a smaller down payment than $1,000, I would have, and my rate of profit would have been even higher. Make the smallest down payment possible. The less you have invested in property, the less it will cost someone else and the faster you can sell.

This applies to your home as well as investment property. Buyers would rather assume a mortgage than get a new loan. Usually the existing mortgage has a better interest rate. And by assuming the existing mortgage, a buyer saves certain closing costs—another advantage.

The profit you make on the sale of your home is a profit on what you have paid into it, not what it ultimately would have cost. Once again, that's the principle of leverage.

Use Other People's Money

Some people tend to be very nervous about borrowing money. They tell me they can't get into real estate because they don't have a down payment. Borrow the down payment.

You've Got to Spend Money to Make Money

Lenders will charge 8 percent interest on a loan for a down payment, but you're going to make more than 8 percent. You'll be able to pay the lenders and still have a profit. That 8 percent interest rate is just the cost of doing business. I used money at 8 percent to make the 100 percent on the lot I mentioned earlier. You must be willing to borrow and operate on borrowed capital because it would take too long to save money for a down payment. So prepare yourself mentally to operate on borrowed capital.

Two Important Rules

1) Don't buy land that you have to resell in a hurry. I managed to sell that $3,000 lot fast, but that was an unusual circumstance. Land is like stocks. It doesn't always sell when you want it to, and it's very difficult to eat. I've got some now I'm thinking of farming because that's all I can do with it. But it will sell eventually. It's just sitting there becoming more valuable. If I needed the money to live on, however, I'd be in trouble. Don't take your live-on money and put it into land.

2) Buy property in the path of progress. If you buy in the boondocks, plan to put the property into your estate and pass it on to your heirs. It will take too long to increase in value to be of any use to you. If you want to make money on it yourself, you've got to buy in the path of progress.

Before Buying

You must satisfy two requirements before you buy real estate.

1) You must have good credit established.

2) You must have enough of an income so you can pay interest rates on the loan and perhaps part of the loan principal.

You must have some back-up money to go into this sort of investing. Without it, you probably couldn't get a loan.

Let's say you're going to buy a lot costing $21,000. You'll probably have to put a third down, so that's $7,000. The down payment gets you ownership of the lot subject to a $14,000 mortgage at 8% interest on the unpaid balance of principal, and four equal annual payments of $3,500 on the principal.

At the end of the first year your interest at 8% on $14,000 is	$1,120.
Taxes will probably run less than $200 a year. Let's figure on	150.
Expenses for the first year	1,270.
If you don't sell the property in the second year you will owe interest on $10,500 of unpaid principal, of $840 plus $150 taxes	990.
You will also have paid, with the interest, two payments of $3,500 on principal	7,000.
Your expenses at end of second year	9,260.

That's how much money you need to hold the lot for two years. But you still own the lot and the mortgage is down to $7,000 on a $21,000 lot.

Note that each year the interest you pay on the unpaid principal goes down rapidly:

First year on	$14,000	1,120.
second year on	10,500	840.
third year on	7,000	560.
fourth year on	3,500	280.

In each year, the amount of interest paid is deductible from income tax base, as are the taxes.

This is a very conservative figure, I should add. If you have $5,000 in reserve when you make a $21,000 purchase, you're definitely approaching real estate investing very cautiously. But if you're nervous about your first transaction, the capital in the background may boost your confidence.

Now that you know how much money you need, and presuming your income is sufficient, you're ready for the next step.

Call a Realtor

Don't waste your time looking on your own or answering ads in the newspaper. You might, just might, stumble onto something. It's more likely that you'd be wasting energy. There are four good reasons why you should go to a professional realtor who's involved in the area in which you want to invest: time, capital, information, skill. Your time and capital. His or her skill and information. People who have good bargains usually don't have signs on them. Better spend your time doing something else and let the person who knows the market spend the time required finding availabilities.

Look for a real estate person who is knowledgeable about trends in the area you want, who takes time to sit down and counsel with you about those trends, who's not eager just to push a paper in front of you and have you sign on the dotted line. If you're looking for property in a small community or in the country, you'll probably do well to deal with a local realtor because he or she will know what's happening in that territory.

Discuss your specific needs with the realtor, explaining you want to make a minimum down payment on a reasonable lot in an area where you could expect quick turnover, say in a year. I like things to move annually, especially when a person is making her first real estate investment. Of course you can't be sure it will sell in a year. Real estate can be slow. That's why you need to buy in the path of progress and have your back-up capital.

In a few weeks, sometimes in a few days, the realtor will call you and say she has something she wants you to see. Perhaps you contacted two or three realtors. You may get proposals from each. Go over the costs carefully and determine which offers the lowest down payment for the best investment.

Borrow the Down Payment

Once you make the decision, you need to borrow the money for the down payment. Go to the bank at which you've already established credit. Outline your plan. Ask for the necessary amount of money for six months or a year. Show them you have an income which will allow you to pay your interest. Bankers are primarily concerned about interest payments. Most will extend, that is lengthen, a loan for a period longer than originally agreed, if you pay the interest due. They may also insist on a small reduction of the principal. You'll find this out when you seek your loan.

You may find that one bank won't lend you as much as you need. Borrow whatever they'll lend and make another loan at another bank and even a third if necessary. That's what I did on my first loan.

Buy Immediately

When you get the loan, purchase the property immediately. You don't want to delay once you have the loan because you pay interest from the time you sign the loan contract. Closing on the sale usually takes a month or longer. This interval is a dead period. You're paying out but have no chance of taking anything in. The loss of time can be very detrimental when you're dealing with money, so every day is valuable.

To Sell or Not to Sell

You may want to resell the property immediately, or you may want to hold it for capital gains. Your decision will depend upon your tax bracket. If you're below the 30 percent tax bracket, you can afford to sell immediately.

If you're fortunate enough to be in a higher than 30 percent bracket, you'll want to hold the property for capital gains. You must hold it one year and a day. Otherwise it's considered income and you pay more tax.

I like to put it for sale the very next day. I list it with the realtor who was enterprising enough to find it for me in the first place. If you make a quick sale, you have to pay income tax on the profit but you won't earn enough on the sale to hurt your tax situation.

If the land doesn't sell immediately, you're confronted with payments, the interest on the loan as it comes due, and possibly the second payment on the property itself. That's why I prefer to sell fast and get on to something else.

A favorite investing saying of mine is: *A nimble nickel is better than a slow dime.*

Unless you're in an enormously high tax bracket, you'll probably find that taking all costs into account, you'll do better to sell fast even though you have to pay income tax on the profit. You can take what's left after paying off your loan and, setting aside the sum for income tax, invest in another piece of real estate.

So many good possibilities may turn up when you're looking that you can't resist buying two, and if you can afford it, go ahead. Don't get too far out on a limb, but as long as you have enough back-up money, you're all right.

Real Estate as a Tax Shelter

If you're in a high tax bracket and need a tax shelter, real estate may be your answer. It has two tax advantages:

1) As I mentioned before, you can hold real estate a year and a day and claim capital gains.

2) You can take depreciation on land with buildings on it.

Shopping Centers

One of the best buys in the whole world is a small shopping center of about six stores. They're for sale often. Actually they're not for sale; they're for trade.

Tenants are already in. They pay rent. The rent keeps up the property, pays your accountant or manager and covers other incidentals. You're not hoping to make a profit on the rent. What you want is depreciation to deduct from your income tax.

You talk with the IRS who tell you what they consider the logical rate of depreciation is. Usually on something like a shopping center, they give you 15 to 20 years. You can depreciate the property over that length of time. They allow you to depreciate some property in 10 years. Your aim is to depreciate it as rapidly as possible because the faster you depreciate it, the larger the deduction each year on your income tax. If you get a 10-year depreciation, that means you can take 10 percent of the value of the total property off your income tax for 10 years.

You can depreciate property two ways. *Composite* depreciates the entire structure at the same rate and time. *Component* depreciates each element in the building separately. This gives you bigger depreciation deductions in the early years and faster write-off.

For instance, suppose you buy an apartment house and have a 20-year composite life. You would deduct one-twentieth of the value of the property each year. But if you use the component method, you might deduct the roof in 12 years, plumbing in 15, building shell in 30 years, etc.

When the full depreciation time is up, don't sell the property. It probably has increased in value during the 10 to 15 years you owned it. If you sold it, you'd have to pay a large tax.

Instead, you trade it.

That's why you find so much trading of properties going on. Read the classified ads in the real estate section of your newspaper. You'll find the situation is often as follows:

Two groups of investors will work as a team. One will buy one small shopping center while the second buys an apartment unit. They take their 10 years or so of depreciation. Then they trade the properties to each other. As long as no money changes hands, they aren't considered to have made a profit and don't have to pay income taxes. They're delaying them.

When and if you finally sell for cold cash, you take the profit and pay taxes. Wealthy people rarely sell anything. That's the reason. They're in too high a tax bracket. If they sold, they might have to pay 92 percent tax on the profit.

Apartment Complexes

The next best investment to a small shopping center is a small apartment complex. A six- or eight-unit apartment house is easily managed. It can be lucrative in four ways: tax advantages, equity build-up, cash flow, eventual profit when it sells.

Suppose you bought an apartment project which is just now being built. You could probably write off or deduct most of your investment, thus saving an amount in taxes equal to your tax bracket.

For instance, let's say you're in the 50 percent tax bracket and you're going to put $10,000 into the project. You can write off the $10,000, which means you can deduct 50 percent of the actual cash on your income tax. So you would save $5,000 in taxes. If you're in the 30 percent bracket and put in $10,000 you could save $3,000. In the 20 percent bracket, $2,000.

Besides saving taxes, you'd have the other benefits of apartment ownership, such as a share of the continuing tax deductions, a share of the equity build-up of the capital appreciation, and the monthly cash flow.

If the project was a success, you should get all of your investment back through tax savings alone over a period of a few years. You'd also get an increasing income which is tax free for a long time. And you'd participate in the equity build-up which might return an amount equal to your investment, once more plus your share of the profit, perhaps several times the original investment.

A successful project could return your money many times given good management. Of course there's always a risk. The apartment may not be successful. But the risk involved is the reason you get the tax advantage. Even if the apartment were just moderately successful, you probably still would make money in the long run.

Single House Rental

Normally I don't recommend buying duplexes or single houses and leasing them. They can be a headache. Tenants call at odd hours for everything from replacing windows to changing washers in faucets. But there are exceptions. If you can work out an arrangement with special tenants, you may do well. The following example was given in the *Wall Street Journal*.

A thirty-three-year-old New York professional woman "borrowed" from her retired parents to buy the $30,000 Florida condominium in which they live. Then she rented the place to them. After taxes, both she and her parents keep more in cash than they otherwise would have had.

The daughter is in the 38 percent tax bracket, the parents in the 19 percent.

The woman paid $3,000 in cash and gave her parents a $27,000 twenty-five-year mortgage note bearing interest of 8.75 percent. The parents invested the down payment in a savings certificate which earns 7.75 percent interest. They also have income from the interest on the mortgage note.

Out-going they have only rent.

Previously they paid property taxes, maintenance, and insurance on the condominium. Because they took the standard deduction on their federal income tax return, the state property taxes they paid earned them no tax benefit.

The daughter now pays property tax, insurance, and maintenance. Those costs added to the amount she can depreciate the value of the apartment exceed her rental income. So she is buying the property and renting at a loss. This gives her a deduction on her income tax.

The end result is an increase in money for both the New York woman and her parents. The Internal Revenue Service has checked out the arrangement and says it is legal.

If you can work out a special arrangement of this sort, a single house can be a good investment.

House Renovation

Some people buy old houses and renovate them for resale. This is fine if you are a do-it-yourselfer. If you have to pay for all the labor, you may not come out with enough profit to make it worthwhile. I have a friend who does this on a regular basis. She buys, renovates, and profitably sells about five houses a year. She does the painting, staining, sanding, wallpapering, and light carpentry herself. Since she does this number of houses, she's able to keep a crew working on the heavier repairs.

Diversified Properties

Sometimes you can find good opportunities to pool your money with other people's and go into a tax-sheltered investment. You could buy a diversified portfolio of income-producing properties. The diversification would reduce some of the risks of single property ownership, so tax advantages and tax flow might be lower and the goal more modest.

Orville I. Cox, with E. F. Hutton & Company, told me he offered a diversified program that typically contains one or two apartment projects, three or four well-located shopping centers, possibly two office buildings, and a major regional mall. Because of both geographical and numerical diversification, one project might fail without hurting the overall portfolio critically. The risk of total failure would be much less. The tax advantages also would be less because of the diversification and reduced risk.

Syndicates

Something you'll probably run into sooner or later when investing in real estate is a land syndicate. This is made up of people who pool a certain amount of money to buy property which would be too expensive for any one of them to buy alone. It's something like a mutual fund on a much smaller basis, and they buy land instead of stock.

Many people go into syndicates as a tax shelter. They want to buy something in which they'll take a loss now while their earnings are high. When their peak earning years are past, the property should have increased in value so they can sell it and keep most of the profit instead of paying it to income tax. This is called deferred earnings.

The theory is good but there are problems in syndicates. Usually you can't sell until 100 percent of the investors agree, although sometimes a syndicate is set up so that only 90 percent have to agree. A TV station with which I'm familiar is owned by a syndicate made up mostly of physicians and their wives.

There are only two non-doctors in the group. The station had a loss factor for quite some time, which pleased everyone. Then it began making a profit. They were hysterical. Their taxes are high enough without adding on the station profits. The non-doctors wanted to sell but the physicians and their wives refused because they didn't want to pay the high taxes that would accompany the sale.

You see some of the difficulties involved. Think long and hard before getting into business with a number of partners. It rarely works smoothly.

A Word of Warning

If all your time and energy are taken up with something else, real estate is no place for you. But if you like the land and what is put on it, if you enjoy buying and selling, have fun and make a profit with real estate.

QUIZ

1. If you want your invested money to double in 10 years, how much interest does it have to earn?

    Seven percent.

2. Why isn't a savings account a good investment?

    Because the rate of inflation usually runs more than the interest rate on the savings account, so you lose money on your savings.

3. The interest rate on a four-year Certificate of Deposit is better than on a one-year CD, but I may want my money before four years are up. What should I do?

Buy the long-term one and hope you can leave it there the full time. If you can't, the penalty for cashing it before maturity isn't large.

4. What is the interest rate on most Treasuries?

From approximately six percent to about eight percent depending upon their time of maturity.

5. Why is it better to buy Treasuries through a Federal Reserve bank or branch?

Because you don't have to pay a broker's commission.

6. What should I do before ever investing in the market?

Study the market and activity of business in general. Familiarize yourself with major companies whose shares you want to buy. Look for companies with good management, good records, good products, the right amount of debt and price-earnings ratio. Talk with good authorities and pick a good broker.

7. Is it better to buy preferred or common stock?

You'll probably make more on common.

8. I always thought preferred stocks were best because of their name.

If there's only a limited amount of money to pay stock dividends, preferred stock will be paid. The money may not stretch to cover common stocks. On the other hand if there's a great deal of money, common is paid more than preferred.

9. Fill in the blanks: The greater the ——, the greater the ——.

PROFIT   RISK

10. How do you know when to sell stock?

If it starts dropping consistently, sell it. Also, when you buy the stock, decide how high it should go. When it reaches the point you've set, you may want to sell it.

11. How long do you have to hold a stock for it to be considered a capital gain?

One year and one day.

12.   Why should I buy mutual funds when the author of the book didn't make money on them?

When the author bought mutuals, she knew very little about the market. Now she would aim for investments with a slow but consistent record of growth. The advantage of mutuals is that you don't have to study the market yourself in order to invest. You can leave that to the professional fund managers.

13.   What are the primary advantages of investment clubs?

The pooled funds of members give you more money to invest, and the members can share information so you can learn more faster than if you had to study the same material by yourself.

14.   When buying real estate, should you make the largest or smallest payment possible?

Usually the smallest.

15.   Is it better to use your own money or borrow money for the down payment?

Borrow. Learn to use other people's money.

16.   If you buy a piece of land, what will your expenses be during the first year not counting the down payment?

Interest on the loan and property tax.

17.   It's all right to tie up all your money in real estate because you know you'll sell it very soon. True or false?

False. It may take months or years to sell. Don't tie up live-on funds in real estate.

18.   Land everywhere is valuable so I should buy the cheapest I can find. True or false?

False. Buy in the path of progress. Land in the boondocks may be valuable someday but unless you want to wait 20 years or so for it to appreciate, buy in an active area.

19.   My accountant said I couldn't depreciate real estate.

You can't depreciate land. You can depreciate structures put on land.

20. I'm thinking of buying a rental house. Is this a good investment?

Tenants can be a headache, as can keeping the house rented. If you don't mind worrying about it frequently, you may make money on it. If the house is in good condition and you can trust your tenants to be fairly care-conscious, it can be a good investment.

Money for the Rest of Your Life

*On Pensions and Profit Sharing,
Insurance and IRA*

If you have no pension or profit-sharing plans where you work, or even if you have, you may want to put aside some money in an IRA or Keogh account.

The advantage of these accounts and plans is that you are not only saving for the future but you are putting off paying taxes in your peak earning years. This is called *deferring taxes*.

During peak earning years you make more money than you will when you retire. You may be in a high-income-tax bracket during top earning years and pay anywhere from 25 to 92 percent income tax.

When you retire and stop earning, your income is drastically reduced, and you may pay no tax at all. Wouldn't it be great to have some of that money you were paying in income tax 10, 15, or 20 years ago? Following are some tax-deferred savings plans. You probably can take advantage of one or more of them.

INDIVIDUAL RETIREMENT ACCOUNT (IRA)

The Individual Retirement Account is government sponsored and, broadly speaking, planned for persons who pay federal income tax at a rate of 25 percent or less. You may save up to $1,500 a year or 15 percent of your income, whichever is less. IRA's attractive features are:

• You may deduct the entire amount you put into IRA from your annual income, which lessens your income tax.
• Your money in IRA earns the highest tax-deferred interest allowed by law. In 1977 that was about 7¾ percent.
• You have no more risk of losing your money than you would in a regular savings account (which is virtually none).

An IRA account is more lucrative than a regular savings account because the IRA interest rate is higher, and you have to declare interest on regular savings accounts as income, which adds to your income tax.

If you put $1,500 into your IRA every year for 20 years, your total fund would be more than $74,500. More than half of that amount would be interest. You save about $9,000 in taxes.

When you withdraw money from your IRA account, you do pay tax on it. The idea however is to wait and withdraw it when your high earning years are past, and your taxes are lower.

Keogh Plan

The Keogh plan is used primarily by small businesses, doctors, lawyers, people with few employees. It is aimed primarily at persons in the 25 to 50 percent tax bracket who have no pension plan where they are employed. You put into this plan as much as $7,500 a year or 15 percent of your earned annual income.

To take advantage of the Keogh plan, you must also make proportional contributions for your full-time employees who have been with you three years or longer. A full-time employee is defined as one who works more than 20 hours per week. And should you have a new business and be entering the Keogh plan, you must include all the employees who have been with you since you started in business. When Keogh plans are set up, they must have the approval of IRS. Once given, they are safe for use as set up originally.

IRA and Keogh can be established at your bank or savings and loan companies. If you're interested, talk with officers of one of these organizations. They can give you specific details, advise you on a savings schedule, and more.

Like IRA, Keogh funds are tax deductible, earn the highest

amount permitted by law, and are risk free. A Keogh plan can even be used to invest and trade in common stocks under certain conditions. A bank trustee must be appointed to keep the books and oversee purchases chosen by the fund owner, and the trustee charges a fee. But as long as the fund owner exercises due caution in his purchases, he's allowed to buy securities of his choice. Few banks in the country offer this service as of this writing but if the practice becomes popular, that may change.

IRA and Keogh are two safe tax shelters. Saving in these accounts is like taking money from one of your pockets and putting it into your other pocket and adding the highest amount of interest the law allows.

Company Pension Plans

These plans are also prime tax shelters. They are set up by an employer who sets aside a sum of money each year for investment in a way approved by the U.S. Treasury. You the employee pay no tax on the annual contributions or the build-up of earnings on the invested money until you retire and start withdrawing funds.

Profit Sharing and Thrift Plans

These plans are offered by some companies and they save you tax money. They vary in form but generally a thrift plan consists of money or stock contributed by an employer to which you can if you choose add savings of your own. Often company stock is the contribution but some companies mix common stock with mutual fund shares and others use insurance company or other investment programs that are professionally managed.

You pay no current income tax on either the amount you contribute to the fund or on earnings from the investment. If you made the same investment in the stock market, you'd pay tax on profits.

Some plans allow you to make partial or complete withdrawals of your balances while you're still working or they can be left for retirement.

Profit-sharing programs operate in different ways. In some the employer is the only one who pays into the fund, contributing a percentage of annual profits. In others the employee also contributes.

LIFE INSURANCE

People who are protection oriented don't feel complete without life insurance. To others it is a hateful parasite feeding on fear and dependence. An insurance agent told me of a woman who was so angry because her husband was planning to take out a $200,000 policy that she walked out of the room, slammed the door, and wouldn't return while the agent was present. The same woman called the agent a few years later to find out if her husband, now deceased, had taken out the policy. He hadn't. She had slammed the door on $200,000.

Many financial experts are also anti-insurance because they think people spend too much on life insurance when the money could be more productive in a relatively high-return investment.

My position is midway between the two extremes. Insurance can secure an estate and tide survivors over difficult times, but you shouldn't limit your investing to insurance because you can make a lot more with it somewhere else. The big difference of course is that you may never get around to investing but you will pay your insurance premium.

Forced Savings

Insurance seems to be the best way for some people to save. Tom Q. Davidson (with Alexander and Alexander of Texas), who sometimes helps me in my seminars, told me that traditionally people who fritter away much of their income are heavily insured. The purpose of life insurance is to replace the policy holder financially when he or she dies.

How Much Do You Need?

The amount of insurance you should have depends upon your age, your dependents if any, their age, your condition and capabilities, and the amount and status of the remainder of your estate. Figure out how much your survivors would need without you. Figure out how much you're going to provide them from sources other than insurance. If you come out short, make up the difference with life insurance.

Do Women Need Insurance?

Most women need some life insurance, as do most men, and for the same reasons:

- To pay for final arrangements
- To pay any debts left outstanding at your demise
- To pay taxes which may come due shortly after your demise
- To protect the financial security of heirs if you have any

The first thing survivors need to pay for is final arrangements, unless you qualify for a government service or plan to die at sea. The average cost of a cemetery lot, funeral, and burial runs about $3,000, and costs are rising.

Another important use of life insurance is to pay federal and state taxes when you die. I go into this in more detail in the chapter on wills, but it bears mentioning here. A person's estate consists of home, business, stocks, bonds, property, and the like, none of which can be converted into cash immediately. Oh, you can sell a house, or cash in your bonds or sell your stocks, but if you have to do it quickly, you risk taking a big loss. The government gives you 18 months to pay taxes, but it can pass before you know it. It's very reassuring to know your heirs won't have to sell something to pay taxes if your insurance is available for that purpose.

If you're married, presumably you'll inherit most of the estate when your husband dies. Taxes aren't too bad when the first spouse dies. The big tax bite comes at the death of the surviving spouse. To preserve an estate for heirs, you may want to buy enough insurance to cover federal taxes at your death.

Also, if you expect to inherit from your parents, you would be well advised to determine what their tax and debt situation is. If you have only one surviving parent and he or she is aging, you may want to take out extra insurance for him or her. Once you have the facts and figures, talk with your insurance agent to determine the proper action to take. If you expected to inherit from a person who has incurred business or personal debts, you may find insurance a logical way to pay them.

If You're Single

An increasing number of single women are buying insurance, according to the American Council of Life Insurance, as the proportion of women ages twenty-five to twenty-nine who remain unmarried has climbed, up more than a third since 1960. Between 1965 and 1975, the average amount of life insurance bought by single women increased 119 percent.

If you are single with no children, no parents who rely on you for income, no sisters, brothers, or other loved ones to whom you wish to leave more than memories, no estate subject to federal or state taxes and no debts, you can limit your life insurance to final arrangement expenses. Considering inflation, I'd recommend a $10,000 policy just to be on the safe side.

When Should You Buy?

Better to buy before you're thirty-five. Premiums are lower the younger you are, assuming your health is good. If you wait too long, you run the risk of being refused insurance because of health problems. Also if you have a cash value policy (I'll explain that term later), you can be accruing assets with your insurance.

Married

If you're married and don't have a job, you may think there's no reason to have insurance because your death would cause no loss of income to your husband. There would still be the need, however, to pay final arrangements and perhaps taxes. And you may realize you need insurance in the future when it would be hard to buy.

If your husband is your primary source of income, you should make sure his life insurance is enough to cover his funeral and burial, any debts he may have, taxes, and enough to keep you going comfortably until you're ready to become self-supporting. How long that will take depends, of course, upon your age, health, career qualifications, and inclinations.

Own Your Husband's Policy

Wives should *own* their husband's insurance policies *and vice versa*. Otherwise the policy is considered part of the estate and counted among assets when the policy holder dies, which makes the tax bill larger. You may save quite a bit of money by owning your husband's policy.

Pay for it with your own money. It isn't sufficient simply to pay for it from your joint checking account even though you sign the checks. Pay the premiums from your own checking account. That way the IRS can never argue that actually the insurance is part of the estate.

If a spouse has no source of income adequate to pay for the insurance, the wage earning spouse can make a gift of enough money to take care of the policy each year. The amount of the gift should not be the exact amount of the premium because the IRS then might maintain that actually the wage earning spouse paid for the insurance.

If you and your husband have policies already in existence, you can make gifts of them to each other and pay any remaining premiums from your own account. Contact your insurance agent and talk with him about how to make the change in ownership. The procedure varies in different states.

Married with Children

If you're a wife and mother, there's another reason for you to have insurance. If you died, your husband would probably have to hire people to take care of the children and the house, do the shopping, cooking, mending, and the hundred and one other things you do. His expenses would mount and the insurance money might see the children and him through some difficult years—and just maybe keep him from making a too precipitate second marriage.

Dependent children send the amount of insurance needed skyrocketing. The principal wage earner in the family should make certain he or she has enough coverage to get the children through school in case of his or her demise.

Divorced

If you're divorced and have no children, you still may want to buy a policy on your husband, naming yourself as beneficiary. There's no law that says you still have to be married to a man to collect his life insurance. Or you may request ownership of an existing policy in your divorce settlement. Normally you would pay the premiums in both cases, although husbands sometimes continue to pay for an existing policy.

If you're divorced and have children, you should make sure your former husband keeps his life insurance in effect and names the children beneficiaries. This is only reasonable since presumably he is paying child support and if he dies the payments would end. If he's the kind of man who's lax about such things, if you can't depend upon him to pay his premiums, better check on them yourself. If he hasn't paid on time, ask his agent to stay after him until he does. Good agents should be happy to cooperate because they don't like to see policies dropped.

Do Children Need Insurance?

Premature death doesn't happen often, thank goodness, but it does happen. I think anyone who drives a car or a motorcycle should have life insurance. Since most people begin driving at sixteen, they should have insurance when they're sixteen. Parents can add riders on their own life policies for a small amount of money.

Updating

Review your insurance policies at least once a year because as your life changes, so may your insurance needs. Maybe your policy was adequate ten years ago but inflation has cut its value in half. Or perhaps you had another child, or you're now helping support an aging parent. If you find the insurance is now inadequate, buy more even though the cost will be greater because your husband is older. It's still good value for the money.

Suppose however you have a tidy sum coming in each year from investments, enough so that your heirs could live comfortably if you died. In that case don't worry about more life insurance. The object is to have enough income from all sources, not just from insurance.

Causes for Refusal of Insurance

The major cause of refusal is heart disease. Also surgery to remove cancer within the past five years will cause refusal from most companies. If you should be refused by a company, however, don't give up. Your agent probably can shop around and find another company who will insure you. Only 3 percent of persons requesting life insurance are refused because of health reasons. However, if your health isn't all it should be, you'll probably have to pay more.

The other reason you may be refused insurance is if you are in a high-risk occupation. Insurance companies shy away from insuring construction workers on 30-story buildings. They're also nervous about weekend pilots and scuba divers.

Assuming you're hale, hearty, and not employed on the high girders, what kind of insurance should you buy?

TERM INSURANCE

The least expensive life insurance is called "term," because it lasts for a specified amount of time. Typically it runs one, five, ten or twenty years, or you can buy term that lasts until you reach a certain age. It has death benefits only. Its only function is to pay your beneficiaries if you die while you have the policy. If you need a lot of coverage but have limited finances, term is what you need to buy.

Costs vary, so shop around. Besides cost, consider the security of the company and look for a helpful agent. He can be a real boon over the years.

Different kinds of insurance cost different amounts depending upon your age, health, sex, occupation, and the companies' experiences with same. Not all companies have the same experiences, which points up that the statistics aren't infallible. If they were, all companies would agree on whether or not so-called high risks should be insured. They might get closer together on costs too.

A term insurance policy should include the following clauses:

- The insurance is renewable regardless of your health
- The policy is convertible to a whole or straight life policy

WHOLE OR STRAIGHT LIFE

As you grow older, you'll probably want to switch from term to a straight or whole life policy, which can come in many different forms. This pays death benefits and remains in effect as long as you pay the premiums, as does the term. But the straight life also builds up a cash value over the years. You don't have to die to get something out of it.

The higher the face value of the policy, the more the premiums, the faster the cash value will grow. If you have an average size policy, you might have $2,000 in ten years, or $4,000 in twenty years.

With cash value, you can

1) Use it to pay future premiums on your policy.

2) Use it to switch over to a different policy, although switching policies is a risky thing, so be sure you know exactly what you're doing. Discuss it thoroughly with your agent.

3) Borrow the cash value at a low rate of interest. Actually you don't even have to pay it back, although if you don't, it will be deducted from the amount paid your beneficiaries when you die.

4) Some policies allow you to use the cash value to pay the premiums as they come due. You can set this up with your agent so the premiums are paid automatically.

5) Leave the $4,000 intact until you're sixty-five and then use it for a retirement fund.

6) Cancel the policy entirely and they'll give you the cash value.

Of all the possibilities, I'd recommend leaving it where it is to accrue, and to have it available for borrowing should you care to. Using it to pay future premiums is sensible also.

A whole life policy contract should include the following provisions:

1) If you become disabled, the company will pay your premiums until you're sixty-five.

2) If your premium isn't paid within 31 days of being due, the payment will be taken out of the cash value of the policy (providing enough cash value has accrued).

3) You may buy additional life insurance in the future without medical examination.

The cost of straight life varies greatly. In figuring the overall cost, you have to take into account the cash value that accrues. An added complication in figuring costs is that there are two kinds of insurance companies, mutual and stock, also called participating and non-participating. A mutual company pays dividends to its policy holders if business is reasonably good. The dividends aren't guaranteed but usually you can count on them. As the dividends accrue, they may reach the point where they're sufficient to pay the premium, so you in effect have a paid-up policy, which remains in effect until you die. This doesn't happen overnight, you understand. It takes more than 15 years. A stock company does not pay dividends but usually its premiums are lower.

The Joint Special Committee on Life Insurance Costs, made up of appointed representatives from the industry, developed a way of figuring the cost of a policy called the Interest-Adjust Method. It factors in such variables as accruing interest, future cash values, and average dividends if any. Putting it all together, they came up with interest-adjusted index numbers. The index number gives a comparison of the cost of one policy with another. Low index number equals low cost policy.

The annual premium cost isn't the only thing to consider in the overall cost of a policy. The index number varies between companies and between policies. One company's lowest index number may be for a woman of twenty-five buying $20,000 worth of straight life while a different company may have the lowest for a woman of thirty-five buying $40,000. You can check *Best's* to get the index numbers (see below) or ask your agent to dig them out for you.

HOW TO CHECK COSTS, COMPANIES AND AGENTS

Check the financial security of any insurance company in a book called *Best's Insurance Reports—Life/Health,* which is probably available at your library. *Best's* two highest ratings are "most substantial" and "very substantial." Either one should do. A company that receives a lesser rating probably would not be for you.

Best's also tells you how much companies charge for different kinds of insurance at different ages of policy holders. Suppose you're twenty-five and want to buy term insurance, you can look through *Best's* and see which companies charge the least. Then check the financial ratings of those companies which charge the least, and go from there.

Most people don't do this sort of checking, of course. They have a friend or relative who sells insurance or they ask a friend who has a good policy or agent. That's the easiest route and it usually works, although it wouldn't hurt to take an hour to examine *Best's*.

I'd recommend you talk to three agents before making a firm decision. Your insurance agent may become very important in your life. He can help you set up an estate plan. Eventually he may know more about your financial affairs than your attorney, so pick someone whose knowledge and ability you respect, someone you can trust and be comfortable with. If you get the feeling he has his interests instead of yours at heart, go to somebody else.

Ask how long he trained before beginning to sell insurance. Some training periods last several months, while others are as short as two weeks. Many agents belong to insurance agencies dealing with a variety of companies. If you have a personal acquaintance you'd like to buy from, ask if he represents any of the companies you picked from *Best's*.

Term or Straight Life?

Straight or whole life is a better investment than term. You pay more but you get more. When I say it's a better investment, I don't mean you're going to make 8 or 10 percent on your money. I mean you're going to have death benefits assured, while at the same time making a little bit of interest on the money you paid to the insurance company.

I recommended that you buy term when you're young because most young people are short of money and need to keep expenses down. However, if you're doing well financially, go ahead and buy whole life.

Be careful however about the amount of your premiums. Suppose you're single at twenty-five, making a good salary, and you commit yourself for $500 worth of insurance each year. Maybe in five years you'll be married, have a baby, decide not to work for a few years and find it difficult to keep up with the $500 payments. If you have to drop a relatively new policy which has built up no cash value, you lose everything you've put into it, so keep your premium payments at a reasonable sum from the beginning.

Term Riders

Obviously you need the most money when you have dependents. If you have a whole life policy, you can add what's called a term rider to it. That means you can buy more insurance and time it to last as long as the children are dependent. It's cheaper to add a rider to the policy you already have than to buy a separate one.

Cover Debts

You can do the same thing to cover other costly things, the mortgage on a house for instance. If you're buying a home but don't want your children to be left with the mortgage and no way to pay it if you should die, you can buy term insurance that will last as long as the mortgage. It's best to do this through your own agent and not through a policy the mortgage company has available.

You can buy either a level or decreasing term policy. The latter decreases in value as time goes on, while level remains the same. If you took out decreasing term to cover the mortgage, the value of the policy would be dwindling along with the mortgage. The premiums remain the same but decreasing is still cheaper than level term.

If you're making a big loan that your survivors would have to pay off in case of your death, you can also buy enough term insurance to cover it.

ENDOWMENT

The third major type of life insurance is endowment. If you buy a $10,000 policy, it will pay you $10,000 at a specified time. Say you want that amount in 10 years. If you die before the 10 years are up, the $10,000 goes to your beneficiaries. If you live, you get it.

The primary disadvantage of endowment is that it's very expensive. Besides, a whole life policy will give you almost the same benefits for a lot less money.

ANNUITIES

The purpose of an annuity is to make sure you, or whoever the annuity is for, have income at a specified time. Its death benefits are negligible.

Suppose you're fifty-five, single, and you've figured out how much money you're going to have at sixty-five and it's not enough. You can buy an annuity to supplement your income when you reach retirement age. You could do the same thing with investments but sometimes people get tired and don't want to take the trouble to keep up with investments. The income from an annuity will not reduce your income from Social Security.

Kinds of Annuities

Annuities come in a variety of forms.

- Some pay on a monthly basis
- Some pay a lump sum at a particular time
- Some begin paying as soon as you buy them
- Others pay sometime in the future
- Some stop paying upon death of the annuitant
- Others pay the balance of the annuity to a beneficiary
- Some pay more than two persons and decrease in payments if one of the annuitants dies

The annuity that pays the most for the money you put into it is a straight-life annuity—it pays an income to you for life and stops when you die.

You can buy an annuity with regular payments over a period of time, the same way you buy insurance. Or you can pay for it in one lump sum. The primary disadvantage of an annuity is that it costs a great deal.

GROUP INSURANCE

Something that's not so expensive is a group insurance policy. If you work where group insurance is offered, take advantage of it. Usually your employer pays for all or part of the premiums. If you leave your job, you lose the benefits of the insurance, although with some group plans, you can convert to an individual policy regardless of your health. The premium payments go up if you do, of course.

Whatever kind of policy you buy, plan to pay the premium only once a year. You can save between 2 and 6 percent of the premium cost by paying annually instead of quarterly or monthly. Don't forget to budget for it each month so you won't have a walloping big expense once a year which wrecks your budget. Or you can make arrangements with most banks to pay your insurance premium. Each month they take out of your account an amount equivalent to your monthly insurance premium. They send a receipt showing what they've done and the whole thing is taken care of.

Where to Keep Policies

Keep the policies AT HOME in a safe place and make sure your heirs know where they are. One of the first things survivors need to do is contact the insurance agents and file claims. If you keep the policies away from home, survivors may have a long delay before they can obtain them. To be doubly safe, make copies of the policies, or list policy numbers and put the list in your safe deposit box. The policies at home could be burned, stolen, or mislaid.

How to Collect

A beneficiary can collect life insurance by sending proof of death and the policies to the agents. The company may also need the birth certificate of the deceased, so keep a copy along with the policies. Before trusting the policies to the mail, beneficiaries should list the numbers to make replacement easier if they're lost.

Pro and Con

Let's review the pros and cons of life insurance. On the Pro side:

1) Life insurance gives you funeral costs.

2) It protects your heirs financially.

3) You can use your life policy for loan collateral at a bank or savings and loan. The insurance company too will lend money at low interest using your policy as collateral.

On the Con side:

1) You tie up money which could be used for investment.

2) The interest rate on your insurance is low compared to a good investment.

But there's always the human element to think about. Perhaps you think you have so much income from other sources that you don't need life insurance, but is that other income as secure as you think? Even large estates may find that in the crunch they need life insurance as cash in hand to pay debts and taxes. To be safe, buy some insurance. But don't spend all your investment money on it.

HEALTH INSURANCE

Everybody needs health insurance to pay for the big medical bills that could wipe you out financially.

A brief trip to the hospital for a breast biopsy can cost $600 to $800. That's if the lump is benign and you spend only a couple of days in the hospital. You can hardly check into a hospital for less than $400. Everything you touch has a price tag.

What Kind of Policies Do You Need?

You need a *basic policy* that covers limited hospital, surgery, and physician fees.

You need a *major medical policy* to cover the cost of a long illness or lengthy recovery.

If you have dependents or no other source of income, you need a *disability policy*.

Basic Policy

This policy pays

- a certain amount for your hospital room for a certain number of days; the specific amount and number of days depends upon the policy
- usually for medical supplies given you in hospital
- sometimes for pre-admission testing, prescription drugs and nursing care at home after you leave the hospital
- a certain amount for surgery
- physician's charges

Basic health insurance is a deductible type of insurance. You may pay for the first $500 of expenses with the insurance company paying remaining bills. Most companies have a "stop loss" feature which means they won't pay more than a certain amount during any given year.

Avoid

Your basic policy should cover a reasonable number of days in the hospital. Don't let anyone talk you into buying a policy that pays for 365 days a year in the hospital. Nobody stays there that long. In fact you have to cling to your bed and have palpitations to stay a day longer than the doctor thinks necessary. Women are up and out three days after childbirth, five after major surgery, ten after something like spinal surgery. Three weeks in a particular year is as long as the average person will ever stay.

Major Medical

Major medical insurance picks up where the basic policy stops. It is intended to take care of extended illnesses or a series of operations.

This also is a deductible insurance. The higher the deductible, the lower your premiums. That is, if you pay the first $100 of your medical bills and the insurance company pays the remainder, your premiums will be higher than if you paid the first $250 and the company paid the remainder. If you can absorb medical bills of $500 or $700 without too much strain on your budget, buy that amount of insurance. Keep your premiums down and stay healthy. You save money by paying premiums annually, as you do with life insurance, so budget accordingly and pay only once a year.

You should buy $20,000 to $50,000 worth of coverage. As you approach retirement, it's wise to increase coverage to $100,000. Some companies urge you to buy hundreds of thousands of dollars' worth of major medical, and almost nobody needs that much. If you had a health problem which was that expensive, you'd probably be disabled and consequently some expense would be paid by Social Security, Workmen's Compensation, or some other plan. Elderly persons receive partial payment from Medicare.

Disability

Disability insurance pays you for loss of income. You can buy it for varying lengths of time—the average is five years—and varying amounts up to 60 percent of your income. It can start at different lengths of time following an illness or accident. It's important to have and too many people ignore it because they simply don't expect to become disabled.

If you should become disabled, you may qualify for Social Security payments or a state Workmen's Compensation plan. Many employers continue to pay your salary or a portion of it if you're disabled. If you have been in military service or belong to a union, you may qualify for some form of payments. But any one of these sources probably would be inadequate if it constituted your entire income. Therefore you need some disability insurance.

The average disability policy pays you for five years, although you can buy it to cover only a few months. You can buy enough to pay 60 percent of your income or less. It can start the minute you become ill or have an accident but your premiums will be less if you delay disability payments until the longest possible period after the beginning of your illness or accident.

Group Health Insurance

If you can buy insurance through your work, union, or a fraternal organization, do so. It's 15 to 40 percent cheaper than private insurance. If you buy it through your place of employment, your employer may pay up to 100 percent of the premium costs.

You have no control over what's covered in a group plan. On the other hand, the company insures you without checking your health, and the insurance can't be cancelled unless you leave the group.

If you're on a group policy and leave your job, you may be able to convert to an individual policy if you stay with the same insurance company. But read the new contract carefully. Usually the benefits are much less for an individual than for a group. You probably will find it preferable to go to another company that specializes in individual coverage.

Extended Benefits

Health coverage usually can be extended to cover your spouse and children.

If you're married and both you and your husband can join group plans, it probably will be cheaper if you both join on an individual basis rather than extending family privileges to each other. Besides, if you have family coverage on a group plan and the insured dies, survivors usually lose coverage. It's better to have your own and be protected.

If you have children, examine the two group policies and decide which one offers the best coverage for them. It isn't mandatory that the father carry the children on his group insurance. However, in case of divorce it is customary for the father to pay health insurance for the children.

Watch For

1) The length of time you must have the insurance before you receive pregnancy coverage.

2) Are children insured from birth? They should be. Many infant problems are discovered at birth or within three days so coverage should begin from the moment of birth.

3) If you are a homemaker and your husband is in a group plan, check to see if the policy has any provision for benefits if you are disabled.

Private Companies

If a group plan isn't available to you, or if you find it inadequate, you'll need to buy from a private health insurance company. Blue Cross is probably the best known, but most major companies offer health insurance. When you're checking *Best's* for life insurance, take time to look at health insurance companies too. They're rated as to security of the company, which is very important because an alarming number of health insurance companies go out of business. *Best's* also shows how much the company has paid out in claims.

QUIZ

1. I already have a savings account at the bank. Isn't that as good as an IRA fund?

No. Interest rates are higher on IRA and Keogh. Also savings accounts are considered income and taxed. IRA and Keogh are not.

2. Is it better to take part in my company pension plan or to take the money I would put into that and invest where I might receive a higher return?

It's impossible to say what the difference might be within 20 years. I would advise you to take part in any company pension, profit sharing, or thrift plan and do outside investing also.

3. If I buy enough insurance to make sure my children can afford college if I die, I have no money left to invest. What should I do?

Buy a whole life policy taking care of basic needs and a term policy. The term is less expensive, will cover the educational needs, and can be timed to end when the children become independent.

4. I've heard that some insurance policies pay their own way. How does that work?

A cash value is built up in whole or straight life insurance. It's a savings program as well as insurance. When the savings part of the policy reaches an adequate amount, it can be used to pay future premiums.

5. Then maybe I'd do better to put all my investment money into insurance.

Probably not. The interest rate you make on straight life is very small.

6. Then how much insurance should I buy?

Enough to replace your financial contribution to your family if you die. The amount varies with number and age of dependents.

7. I have no dependents. Do I need life insurance?

Yes. To pay for funeral and burial, any debts and taxes at your death.

8.   Is mortgage insurance a good investment?

If you have dependents who will want to keep your home, yes.

9.   Why shouldn't I limit my life insurance to term? It's cheaper.

The cost of term rises as you age. However it still factors out to be economical as compared to other policies. One of the primary advantages of whole life is that you build a cash value which can be used for a variety of things.

10.   How can people call insurance an investment when it makes such a small rate of interest?

Remember that life insurance plays a double function. It has death benefits which are more than common stock offers. You can't expect to make 9 percent on your money and still receive the face value of the policy when you die.

11.   If I bought no insurance but put all my money into the stock market, I might come out better.

You might. But you might not. Insurance involves practically no risk. Better make sure there's something left for your family when you die by buying some life insurance.

12.   Should I buy the cheapest insurance I can find?

Probably not. The lowest premiums don't always mean the least expensive whole life policy. You have to consider cash values and dividends, if any. A good agent is also very important, as is the security of the insurance company.

13.   Should children be insured?

If they do anything risky such as driving an auto. You can add a rider to your own life policy for children.

Money for Taxes

Income tax is our annual payment to the government. It's something of a financial headache, but with a bit of organization, you can reduce a migraine to a minor discomfort. The secret is to plan in advance and follow through. Here are some suggestions for making the figuring easier.

1) Get 12 file folders or manila envelopes.
2) Label them with the names of the months.
3) Every time you make a purchase, note on the receipt what it was for and drop it into that month's folder. When tax time comes, you have all your purchases dated and labeled, ready to deduct if they're deductible or to add up for a sales tax deduction.

TAX SHELTERS

You don't have to be a big time operator to be interested in and have tax shelters. Again I'm quoting Orville Cox of E. F. Hutton & Co. Tax shelters can be risky, profitable, fun, ridiculous, time consuming, boring—even worthwhile. Some kind of tax shelter is available to almost everyone. The most common include:

- your home, if you own or are buying
- pension plans, profit sharing and thrift plans, IRA and Keogh funds
- stock dividends (limited)

The most common tax shelter, and the only one many people ever have, is a home. That's one of the reasons owning a home is cheaper than renting. You can deduct the interest on your mortage as well as property and school taxes from your income tax.

Another tax saving can be taken on stock dividends. The first $100 of dividends from stocks can be exempted from income tax. If you're married and own stocks individually but file a joint return with your husband, each of you can claim $100 in dividend exemption.

HIGH INCOME—LOW DEDUCTIBLES

If your income is high but your deductibles low, perhaps you should look around for one of the following tax shelters:

- small business complex
- small apartment complex
- large apartment complex
- oil and gas drilling
- movie production
- cattle feeding and breeding

A small business is a good tax shelter. It provides deductions on interest on the money borrowed to go into business, depreciation on the building and equipment, salaries of employees, and taxes. (I discuss this more fully in the real estate section of investments.) You not only acquire deductions but increase your equity for profit. A small apartment complex offers the same deductions and advantages. These two tax shelters are relatively low risk.

A large apartment complex is a great deal more complicated and requires more attention and money. The risk factor is still relatively good.

The last three items are different matters. They take lots of capital, although you may get into a joint operation for as little as $10,000. But they're very *high risk*.

WATCH FOR DEDUCTIBLES

Some common deductions are entertainment, both out and at home in connection with business; travel in connection with work and in-town transportation if you are calling on clients or meeting people connected with work. Remember to deduct sales tax, especially on high-cost items such as cars and television sets.

WHAT TO LOOK FOR IN HIGH-RISK TAX SHELTERS

Find out all you can about the people who are managing the operation, their record, their experience, their reputation.

Investigate the type of enterprise. If it's land, go to the library and read everything you can on big land ventures. Some of them are marvelous but some have been enormous swindles. If it's oil, read about oil exploration by independents. What are the percentages of finding oil each time a hole is drilled? I can tell you, the percentages are very small. A lot of holes are drilled which never come close to a drop of gas or oil. On the other hand I have a friend who's drilled eleven holes and only three have been dry. If it's cattle you're thinking of investing in, read about the market. It goes up and down and if it's down for long, you can lose everything.

Talk to a banker. Bankers are very cautious with money and aren't inclined to take risks, so your banker's opinion should balance the sales promotion you receive.

A TAX SHELTER SHOULD SAVE MONEY FOR YOU

A tax shelter is a worthwhile financial maneuver and can save a great deal of tax money. But don't become so obsessed with saving tax money that you forget to save your principal. The object is eventually to make money. The higher the tax savings, the higher the risk. That's why government allows the tax savings, as incentives for people to finance high-risk activities. Don't make the mistake of thinking a venture is a tax shelter when it's a ripoff. Get good professional advice and study the situation yourself before investing.

QUIZ

1. If you don't have at least one oil well, you may as well forget about tax shelters. True or false?

False. Everyone who pays income tax can and should make use of any tax shelters available.

2.   Isn't this cheating the government?

No. Congress deliberately offers tax advantages to encourage people to invest in high-risk enterprises or to make high-cost purchases such as homes available to more people.

3.   What is the most common tax shelter?

Your own home.

4.   What is the second most common tax shelter?

A pension plan.

5.   If your employer doesn't offer a pension, the next best way of saving for the future is a savings account. True or false?

False. Interest on savings accounts are taxed as income. Set up an Individual Retirement Account (IRA) or Keogh plan at your bank or savings and loan company. These draw interest but aren't taxed until you draw out the funds.

6.   If I have to pay tax eventually, why not do it now while I'm earning enough money to pay the tax?

Because if you're earning now, your tax bracket is probably higher than it will be when you retire. You will pay less tax on the savings when your income is less.

7.   Someone told me that even if I lose money on a long-term investment, I'm not losing it because I'd pay it in taxes anyway. I don't understand.

Suppose you're going to pay $10,000 in income tax this year. Suppose you invest and lose $5,000. The investment reduced your income, thereby reducing your income tax to $5,000. You pay $5,000 in taxes, lose $5,000 in investment. You're out $10,000 just as you would have been if you'd paid it all in taxes. The difference is that eventually your investment may return some income to you.

8.   I've been offered a chance to invest in the production of a movie but I've got to let them know if I'm coming in by tomorrow. What should I do?

Skip it. Any time you're investing thousands of dollars, you need plenty of time to investigate the enterprise. If you get a rush act, rush away with your money intact.

The World of Money

Credit, Banks, and Loans

As you progress toward financial independence, you will become involved in the world of money. You need to know a great number of things, including

- your rights concerning credit
- how to establish and maintain credit
- how to choose a bank
- where to make loans
- what kind of security you need to make a loan
- what your legal rights are in making loans

The first step is achieving a good credit rating.

CREDIT

You need good credit because sometime you may have a financial emergency and need to borrow money. Or you may have a fantastic investment opportunity and need to borrow. Without a good credit rating, you can't borrow a red cent. You may have enough stars in your crown to form the Milky Way, but credit agencies aren't interested in stars. They're interested in whether or not you pay your bills. That's what a credit rating tells them.

I spoke at a church in Houston to a group of 200 women. During the intermission a young woman remarked that she and her husband had no credit. They always paid cash. That's a statement I hate to hear, that somebody always pays cash. It strikes terror to my heart. What happens if you run out of cash?

That night, so help me, the husband, who was only twenty-eight, had a heart attack and died. It's the sort of coincidence that is stranger than fiction. The wife and her three little children were left in a terrible fix. She had very little cash, no credit, they had been in town only a short time and there was no will. She was almost destitute before she got everything settled.

At least her difficulties proved to the other women who had attended the seminar that it really was important to have their affairs in order.

Most People Establish Credit By

1) purchasing something on time payments
2) opening charge accounts
3) borrowing money from a bank or other lending organization and repaying it as required

If you're single and have done any of these things, you probably have a credit rating.

It is wise to maintain your credit separately if and when you marry. Remember the sentence from English class, "She and I are a couple and it is I"? That's been the attitude of credit agencies from time immemorial. If a couple established credit, the husband had the rating. Wives usually were termed in credit jargon "non-persons."

Late in 1975 the federal government passed the Equal Credit Opportunity Act which says that a woman must be given equal credit consideration with a man. On the subject of joint accounts it says:

"Creditors must report all information of joint accounts used by both spouses and opened prior to November, 1976, in both names, or advise the husband and wife in writing of their right to have credit accounts opened after November 1, 1976, in the name of both spouses when both spouses use the account or are liable for it."

All of this means that women now have the law on their side, but they may have to go to some lengths to make the law a reality. Lending officials tell me that, regardless of the new law, they find women encountering discrimination in credit matters.

Save yourself a lot of trouble by maintaining your credit if you marry. Either you can keep your charge accounts in your maiden name, or you can write each of your creditors, explain you are to be married, that your married name will be such and such, and that you wish to retain your credit separately from your husband's.

How to Check Your Credit Rating

If you're curious about your credit rating—whether it exists, what it says—you can request a copy from the local credit bureau. The telephone number can be found in the yellow pages under "Credit Reporting Agencies."

In some cities there are several agencies. To determine which one to call, ask the store at which you apply for credit for the name of the unit they use. Or ask your banker, attorney, or the business editor of the newspaper. Usually the other agencies listed in the phone book deal in evaluating businesses, verifying authenticity of claims made by firms, and other things we're not interested in at the moment. If you live in a small town, you may have to apply to a larger town for your rating. Your banker or attorney can advise you.

Call the number and tell the person who answers that you want to check your credit rating. Although I know I have a good rating, I tried this to see what happened. The girl who answered the phone told me to write a letter stating that I wanted to check my credit and to send it to them, enclosing $2. They would then mail my report. I told her I didn't want to know what it was. I simply wanted to know if I had it. She said the same thing, write a letter, enclose $2.

The charge for checking may go as high as $5 depending upon the city.

Negative Rating

Suppose you do have a rating and suppose, horrors, it's negative. That means that professional personnel regard you as a poor credit risk, and you won't be able to even open a charge account. Borrowing money would be out of the question.

First find out why you have that rating. Maybe it's a *mistake*. For instance, suppose you owed the veterinarian $100 for setting your boxer's broken leg when he was hit by a car. Suppose you mailed a check for that amount but it never reached the vet. Perhaps there were phone calls back and forth. You wanted to wait a few days to see if the check arrived. And eventually you forgot the whole thing.

Actually you noticed it each month when you figured your bank balance but you never did anything about it. But the vet did. He turned your name over to the credit rating agency.

Phone immediately and get the matter straightened out. A conversation might go something like this:

CLINIC: *Bow Wow Clinic.*

YOU: May I speak to the bookkeeper, please.

CLINIC: I'll try to help you.

YOU: I'm Anne Mason, and I've just learned I still owe you $100. I mailed a check to you in that amount dated October 5, but apparently it never reached you.

CLINIC: (*after looking up the records*) No, Miss Mason. We received no check. We called you twice about this bill.

YOU: Yes, I know. I must apologize. The matter slipped my mind. I'll mail you a check today and I'll phone again in three days to make sure it arrived.

CLINIC: That will be fine.

YOU: Once it does, I would appreciate your writing the credit bureau and correcting the negative report on my rating.

CLINIC: Certainly. I can do that.

Be sure and follow through. Make certain the check reaches the vet. Make certain they write the letter to the credit bureau. Check the bureau and make certain your rating is corrected. Then your credit is good again.

Remember, even if the report is months old, ask the people who reported you to submit a corrective report to the credit agency.

Maybe the negative rating is justified. You really didn't pay a bill. Suppose you had a couch recovered and the upholsterer made a mistake and covered it in red plaid when you had picked out beige. You were aghast when he returned the couch. You pointed out the mistake but he denied you had specified beige and refused to change the fabric. You in turn refused to pay him. So he submitted a complaint to the credit agency.

In this case you won't accomplish anything by trying to get the upholsterer to change the information. You can however write a letter to the agency explaining the circumstances. They don't remove the negative rating but they attach the letter to the report so prospective creditors can read the explanation.

Occasionally people get negative ratings that are deserved but excusable under the circumstances. If someone in the family was sick and you had extensive medical bills, you may have neglected other bills and received a negative rating. This will stay on the records six years. If you go into personal bankruptcy, it stays on the record 14 years.

You can't do much about the rating in these cases except write a letter of explanation and state that you now are able and willing to pay any bills you may incur. If you don't know what to say, credit bureau people can help you. This letter will be attached to your rating and may help somewhat.

If You Don't Have Credit

If you don't have a credit rating, you can establish it by two simple steps: (1) open a bank account and (2) after a period of time, make a loan from this bank.

If you are married, don't accept any account the bank wants your husband to sign for; open the account in your own name, not your husband's.

What Is Your Legal Name?

If you're single, your name is the one your parents gave you, for instance, Mary Sue Evans.

If you marry a man named Harry Dalbert and take his name, your legal name is

> Mary Evans Dalbert   *or*
> Mary Sue Evans Dalbert   *or*
> Mary S. E. Dalbert   *or*
> Any combination of the name and initials you choose.

Many people think a married woman's legal name is her husband's name with "Mrs." on the front. It isn't. "Mrs." is simply a social title.

Once you've opened the account, do business with the bank for a while and do it well. For goodness sake, don't allow yourself to be overdrawn. If you've opened a savings account, deposit some money in it each month.

It may be a comfort to you to know, if you want to keep your financial affairs to yourself, which most of us do, that savings and checking accounts do not go to credit rating agencies. That's private information between your bank and yourself.

At the end of a reasonable period, you take the second step in establishing credit. You make a loan from the bank.

Making the Loan

You want a short-term loan to run 90 or 180 days. You want it to establish credit. That's the only reason. You may tell the bank officer this. You probably won't be the first woman who's asked to borrow money so that once she pays it back she will have a good borrowing record. But, if you are the first, all the better. It will be a new experience for the loan official as well as you.

If the banker asks for collateral, that is, a savings account or stocks or bonds to be put up as guaranty that the loan will be repaid, tell him you don't want to do business with him. Anybody will lend money on collateral. That doesn't establish credit. An exception to this rule is if you have no source of income. In that case you may have to fall back on assets as collateral to get a loan.

The loan officer, all creditors actually, look for two things when considering whether or not to make a loan: (1) willingness to repay, and (2) ability to repay.

The willingness to repay is established by your credit rating. If your record with the bank is good, that's a big plus in your favor. The loan officer also may consider your stability. He or she may want to know how long you've lived at your present address and how long you lived at your previous address. Generally speaking, stable persons tend to stay longer in one home than the unstable. If you've moved three or four times in the past four years, the loan officer may decide you're a bit unstable.

The ability to repay depends upon your income, which can come from a variety of sources.

Sources of Income

- Salary outside the home
- Alimony
- Child support
- Maintenance
- Husband's income in a community property state
- Independent assets

If you work, even if it's only part-time, you have an income which probably will satisfy a loan official.

If you are divorced, whatever payments you receive from your former husband—alimony, child support, maintenance—are considered as much income as a salary.

If you're married, don't work, and live in a community property state, you should be all right. The law specifies that half of everything a husband earns belongs to his wife, and vice versa. Community property states are Arizona, California, Idaho, Louisiana, Nevada, New Mexico, Texas, and Washington. If you don't live in a community property state, you can work out an arrangement with your husband so he pays you a salary.

If you have no source of income whatsoever, you'll probably have to fall back on collateral to satisfy the ability to repay a loan. You may have an inheritance that can be used as collateral. If you're married, your husband can make you a gift of a piece of property or even a sum of money that can be used as collateral.

Probably you won't be turned down. The loan officer most likely will agree to lend you a reasonable sum. If he doesn't, move your account somewhere else, wait awhile, and borrow money there.

When You've Made the Loan

Once you've borrowed the money, pay it back well before the due date. You asked for a short-term loan, for $1,000 for 90 days. Pay it back in 60 or 70 days. There could be a slight penalty for early repayment, but if so it is well worth it. What you are actually doing is spending a small amount of money to make your credit record at the bank look excellent instead of just all right. Look at it as an investment against the time when you might need a loan in a hurry.

Don't spend a penny of this borrowed money! Granted it seems a waste to have $1,000 and not spend a little, but that's a no-no.

Do not touch that money. If you're extremely susceptible to temptation, put it immediately into a savings account, even in the same bank. Go straight from the loan officer to the teller's window and tuck the money away, safe from your hands. At the end of 60 or 70 days draw the money out of the savings account, pay back the loan and congratulations! You have a good credit rating. (For more details about making loans, see the end of this chapter.)

We're not going to stop with simply a good rating, however. You want to be in a financially secure position. So the next step in preparing yourself is to open at least one charge account in a retail store.

Charge Accounts

You probably have several accounts if you're married but they're probably in your husband's name with "Mrs." preceding. This may not do in a crunch.

If a store refuses you an account in your own name, remind them of the Credit Act. You can't be refused an account simply because you're a woman. If you have a good credit rating and they refuse you, sex can be the only reason. You may have to persist with phone calls and letters, but once credit people see you intend to make an issue of it, they'll give you the account.

Once you have the charge account, be very careful to pay your bills on time. You don't want to sully that good credit rating. It is more precious to you than rubies.

Charge Mistakes

If you find a mistake on your charge account, immediately write the store telling them they are in error and asking for a correction. You can phone but a phone call may be forgotten. It's safer to write. Your letter might go something like this.

Date

Credit Department
Too Casual Department Store
1616 First Avenue
City, State, Zip

Gentlemen:

Today I received my charge account bill, account #34681, and noted that you charged me on June 12 for the purchase of six twin bed sheets. I bought no twin bed sheets. Please deduct the charge of $38.00 from my bill and send me a new statement, excluding this erroneous charge.

Thank you.

Very truly yours,

You have 60 days to write a letter asking that your charge account be corrected according to procedures outlined by the Federal Truth-in-Lending Act. But don't wait 60 days. Do it immediately, before you forget.

The store has 30 days to take some action. At the very least, they must let you know that they received your letter. They must either correct your account or explain why they're right and you're wrong within 90 days. Until something is established, they can't report you to a credit bureau or do anything else to damage your credit.

At the end of this time if the store insists they're right, but you don't agree, write back to them within 10 days. They may still report you to the credit bureau but they must include a copy of your letter denying the charges.

If they do prove right and you have to pay the bill, they may tack on late charges, which you're obligated to pay. So, make sure you're right at the beginning. Make sure no family member used your charge card and forgot to tell you. Then stay after the store politely but persistently until you prove yourself right.

Oil Company Credit Card

If you own a car, you should get at least one credit card for gasoline. You can get an application at your service station. With a good credit rating, you should have no problems. Without it, you could run into difficulties.

Once you have the card, use it once or twice a month. Otherwise it becomes inactive and will be cancelled at the end of a year.

Now You're in Good Financial Shape

When you've earned a good credit rating, opened a charge account at a major store, and obtained a gas credit card if you own a car, you're in good financial shape. You could now stay afloat financially *without cash* for several months if the need should arise.

Now let's go back to the first step where you opened the bank account. Where are you going to open it?

BANKS

Not all banks offer the same services or charge the same amounts. You may be able to save quite a bit of money if you choose the right bank.

- Some banks charge carrying charges
- Some require a minimum deposit
- Some charge every time your balance drops below a stipulated amount
- Some charge for safe deposit boxes

Checking Accounts

There are four basic kinds of checking accounts which vary somewhat with states so you may not find all of these methods everywhere or you may find a variation of them. Your checking account probably will fall into one of these four categories:

- minimum balance
- regular checking
- special checking
- free checking

One guess as to which is the most economical! Free checking accounts are easy to find in some cities, impossible in others. Even if a bank doesn't normally offer free checking, it may if you are a senior citizen or if you have a sizable business account with the bank.

Talk to a bank officer if either of these situations fits you and see what can be arranged.

Minimum balance account: means you have to keep a certain amount in your account below which it may not fall. If it does, you're charged extra. Different banks require different amounts. The minimum balance can be figured two ways.

The average balance method: balances are computed daily, totaled at the end of the month, and divided by the number of business days in the month. If your average balance remains within the specified minimum, you won't be charged even though you fell below the minimum one or two days.

The minimum balance method: the service fee is based on the lowest balance on any day during the month. So you're not allowed to drop below the minimum even one day without being charged.

Obviously the average balance is better for you.

The minimum balance accounts sometimes are advertised as free. They're not completely free, because if you didn't have to keep a balance in your checking account, you could put it into savings and be earning interest. For instance, if you put $200 in a savings account where you earned 5¼ percent interest, at the end of a year you'd earn $10.50, more if interest was compounded. That's $10.50 more than you'd earn in a checking account. Besides, if you fall below the minimum and are charged $2 each month, you're spending $24 on your "free" checking account.

Special checking accounts often have a fixed monthly service charge, usually $1.00 or less, plus a fee for each check written, usually about ten cents a check. The ten cents usually is charged for deposits as well as checks. If you write only a few checks each month, this can be a fairly inexpensive account. If you write several, it costs money.

A regular checking account is something like a minimum balance account. You're charged only if your balance falls below a certain amount, although you have to pay for having your checks printed. The bank normally allows you to write a few checks or make a few deposits without charging, but if you write more than their limit, they charge five cents or ten cents per transaction. Like the minimum balance account, the regular checking account can be figured two ways and the average balance method is better for you.

Which Is Better?

The free account costs the least. The regular checking account is probably next best—if you don't write many checks and don't fall beneath the set minimum. If you write numerous checks, the minimum balance account figured on an average balance method would be better. Again this is true only if you stay above the minimum. The most expensive account normally is the special checking.

Time Lapse on Deposits

Banks are in business to make money, and they don't like risks, so they sometimes hold your deposit slip if it's written on another bank until they make sure the funds really are available. For instance, you may deposit funds from AB bank into XY bank. You note the deposit in your checkbook and assume that's how much money you can spend. But don't spend it for a few days. The money may not be there. The bank may not credit your account with the deposit until they actually receive the okay from the other bank.

It can take up to six business days to get the funds into your account if the two banks are in the same town. If they're states apart it could take up to two weeks. However, if you have a record of satisfactory transactions with your bank, most will give immediate credit on checks drawn on another bank. Better check if you make a deposit and need the funds immediately. Ask the teller or an officer of your bank about their procedure.

Free Checks

Another way you can save money with a bank is to get free checks. Not all banks offer them, but some have free blank checks that are not imprinted with your name and address. Or some will print 200 checks with only your name and account number at no charge. Most stores won't accept checks without your address as well as name so you could buy a rubber stamp and do the checks yourself. The most expensive checks you can buy are the pretty ones with pictures on them.

Free Mailing

Ask for envelopes addressed to your bank. Most banks carry them. This saves both your money and the time taken to look up the bank's address and write it.

Safe Deposit Boxes

Another way you can save money is on safe deposit boxes. Some banks and savings and loan companies offer free boxes if you have an account with them. If you can't find a free one, pick the least expensive one that is most convenient to you.

Married persons probably will take a joint box. Make sure the account reads "Wife's Name OR Husband's Name," not "AND Husband's Name." "OR" is the key word. It would take both signatures every time you wanted to get into the box if it were listed AND.

If you keep cash in the box, you have to have a written agreement with the bank from the beginning that if one of you dies, the surviving spouse may withdraw the cash. Otherwise you have to obtain approval from the executor of the estate and communicate formally with bank officials. In the event of the death of one of the box holders, the box is sealed or tagged. Getting into it after that can be a problem even if you don't have cash in it.

When my mother died, we knew death was imminent so about a week ahead I went to the safe deposit box, which I held jointly with her and my father, and took everything out. About three days after her death, I wanted to return some of the material to the box so I went to the bank and asked for the key. It wasn't in its place. I explained there had been a death of one of the three box holders.

The bank employee assembled four persons including himself to act as witnesses as I opened the box. If it had not been empty, if it had contained something I wanted to remove, I would have been refused until an inventory was made and approval to remove was obtained. I sympathize with the bank's need to protect its box holders, but it's easier for everyone if you remove box contents before the box is sealed or tagged.

Avoid Joint Accounts

Spouses think they're safeguarding each other's interests by opening joint banking accounts. Actually the opposite is true because if a spouse dies, the account can be frozen. The remaining spouse can't touch a penny of it until the estate is settled, which may take months or years.

The first claim against an estate is debts. The second claim is taxes. A bank will hold your account until debts and taxes are paid. If you ask a banker about this, he'll say they always pay joint accounts. But he's not taking debts and taxes into consideration.

A friend of mine operated a store along with her husband. He became ill and spent two years in the hospital before he died. They hired a manager to operate the store during the illness. Sales tax was collected by the store but the manager overlooked sending it to the government. The owners didn't realize it wasn't being paid.

The couple had three joint banking accounts, one primarily his, one primarily hers, and one for business. After the husband died, the widow wrote several checks and every one bounced. She was naturally upset and phoned the bank, thinking someone had made a mistake.

She learned the state had frozen all three accounts and they stayed frozen until she paid the delinquent state tax. It took quite a while to figure up how much she owed after two years of business. If she had had one of those bank accounts in her own name instead of jointly with her husband, she would have had some cash for expenses while she was getting together the tax payments.

If you separate from your husband, you should immediately close all joint accounts. This protects both of you from bills the other spouse might incur.

There are a thousand reasons why you shouldn't have a joint bank account. I wouldn't have a joint account with St. Peter if he told me I had to have it to get inside the gate.

Old Bank Accounts

If you left a bank account in your home town when you moved, don't leave it too long. It could be closed. Accounts languish all over the country drawing interest from which nobody will ever benefit because their owner is dead and the heirs don't know about them. Some people put money in banks under different names. W. C. Fields is reported to have done this. I have a friend who says her grandmother did. She told her daughter she had several accounts in other names but she didn't say what the names were. Two years before her death, she had a paralytic stroke. She could neither talk nor write, and the accounts were lost as completely as if they'd been tossed into the ocean.

If a bank account isn't used—no deposits, no withdrawals—for seven years, banks try to find the owner at the last known address. If he's not there, they carry on the search throughout the city or area. Once a year all accounts which have been inactive for seven years are listed in a local newspaper. Bank officials wait a reasonable length of time—what's considered reasonable varies—but if nothing is heard from the account owner or his heirs, the money is turned over to the state. If the owners or heirs turn up after this, the bank has forms which can be filled out to petition the state for return of the funds.

SHOP FOR MONEY

Doesn't that sound like fun? You may have shopped for many things but probably never for money. There's a whole world of bargains out there waiting. If you're the kind of woman who hates shopping, think of it this way. You don't have to try anything on and it's not going to fade in the wash. If the economy behaves, it won't even shrink.

All institutions charge a certain amount for the money they lend, called interest. It's like charging rent for the money while it's out of their hands.

It is a certain percentage of the amount lent. It varies according to federal law and with the individual lending agency. Interest rates can vary from 5 percent to 30 percent annually. The precise amount varies by states and institutions.

The people who charge 30 percent won't come right out and say it's 30 percent. They say they're charging, say, 18 percent. But there are tricky little clauses in the contract, like a service charge of 3 percent. That doesn't look like much, but 3 percent of $1,000 is $30. Or maybe there's a mandatory insurance premium in the contract. Again, the overall cost of the loan increases.

You don't have to try to figure out the complex terms of the contract. To know exactly how much interest you will pay, ask the *Annual Percentage Rate (APR)*. That includes every charge in the contract. If you ask, the lender is required by law to tell you this amount. You'd better get it in writing so if the worst should happen, it won't be a case of your word against his.

Where to Look

When shopping for money, you can go to

- banks
- savings and loan firms
- insurance companies
- finance companies
- family and friends

Lending institutions vary somewhat by state but most of them are found in all states.

Banks and Savings and Loan companies. They lend money for almost anything and in almost any amount, depending upon whom they are lending it to. They're nice people, for the most part, so you can depend upon them to be fair. They're also highly regulated by federal and state governments. Not all banks lend money at the same rate of interest so in shopping for money, it may be necessary to call several.

Bank credit cards. If your bank offers its own credit card and you have one, you usually can borrow money with no problems. The interest rate usually is 12 percent. Some banks, however, add a transaction fee which can run the APR to 36 percent during the first month of the loan. This kind of interest rate is not something you want to pay, and in many areas of the country is not a legal rate.

Insurance companies lend money using your life insurance policy as collateral. The APR is from 5 to 8 percent on the outstanding balance until the principal is repaid. That's about the best interest rate going. A person can even borrow the money from the insurance company without repaying the principal of the loan. Of course if the principal isn't repaid, the amount of money the policy pays when it's cashed is reduced commensurately. If you borrow money against your life insurance policy and die before it's repaid, your beneficiaries will receive the face value of the policy less the amount borrowed plus interest to date of death. If you own your husband's policy, you will have to make the loan.

Finance companies are the ones who advertise they'll lend any amount. They probably will. And do you pay for it! If you borrow, say, $500 for six months, you may wind up paying back $650. That's the 30 percent interest rate mentioned before. That is not a very good deal. If you must do business with a finance company, you should make sure they don't compound interest daily. But it is better to avoid them like the plague.

Credit unions are good to borrow money from if you happen to belong to one. Credit unions are cooperative associations of people who work for the same company or belong to the same organization. They have savings accounts in the credit union; consequently money can be borrowed from it. The types of loans vary, as they do with banks. Interest rates also vary between approximately 9 and 12½ percent.

KINDS OF LOANS

Consumer installment loans are available from banks and savings and loan institutions. Loans are made in amounts that depend upon your income and savings. They are used for various things including home improvements and car buying. They have a fixed time limit, usually one to three years, and are repayable monthly. Interest rates vary between 10 and 20 percent depending on the type and amount of the loan, your credit rating, and the bank's own policy.

If you repay an installment loan early, you may be penalized because the bank loses the additional interest they would have earned if you had paid for a longer period. They've had extra paperwork too. They may

1) charge by the "actuarial method" which measures the exact amount of credit you had used computed at the APR disclosed on your credit contract

2) charge a flat amount of a percentage of the loan outstanding

3) charge by the "rule of 78's" or "sum of the digits" method. The rule of 78's costs you more than any of the others.

Make sure you understand what is involved before you ever make the loan. Ask questions, and then ask again if you're not certain you understand.

Passbook loans are available from banks and savings and loans. A form of installment loan, these tend to be the cheapest way to borrow. Your savings account is collateral and you can't borrow more than the amount in your savings account. And, of course, you can't take any money out of your savings account until the loan is paid. It does, however, continue to earn interest. So, if you're paying 7 to 9 percent for the loan itself, and the savings account is earning 5½ percent, the real interest on the loan is 1½ to 3½ percent. This kind of loan doesn't show up on your credit history, and you'd have to convince yourself of the logic of having on deposit the amount you want to borrow from the bank. Sometimes you can justify it.

If you should default on (not repay) a bank loan, the bank can repay itself from your checking and/or savings account. This is called a "right of offset."

Secured loans are available from banks and savings and loan companies. These are guaranteed by some collateral just as the passbook loan is secured by the money in your account. Loans may be secured by stocks, bonds, or real estate. If you want to make a loan to buy a car, you may get it cheaper if you secure the loan with stocks or bonds than if you offer only the car itself as collateral.

Insurance loans may be made through banks or your insurance company. Banks lend money against the cash value of insurance. The bank holds the policy and doesn't return it until the loan is repaid. When you borrow against the policy from the insurance company which sold you the policy that company simply deducts the unpaid balance of the loan and any interest due from the face of the policy when payment of the policy is to be made.

Mortgage loans are available from banks, savings and loans, insurance companies, and mortgage companies. Loans are made in amounts which depend on your income and savings. Interest is regulated by the federal government and has been climbing steadily, with a few temporary sags backward, for several years.

It is difficult for a woman to get a mortgage alone simply because she usually hasn't enough income to qualify. I discuss this more fully in the chapter on homes. If you are single, want to buy a home, and don't have sufficient income, you might be able to swing a loan if someone co-signs.

If you're married and work, your income can be added to your husband's if you're buying a home jointly. 'Twas not always so. This is part of the Credit Act. Until it was passed, lenders rarely considered a woman's income because they suspected she would be quitting work to have babies or to take care of the ones she already had. A lender is not allowed now to ask whether you plan to have children. He is required simply to consider the amount of your salary with no questions asked.

Which Is Best?

Looking at these different types of creditors and loans, it's obvious which is worst: the finance companies. The best? Insurance companies, banks, savings and loans, and credit unions, depending upon which one will give you the best interest rate when you want to borrow.

There are other kinds of loans where you don't actually go and take away money. Instead you buy an item and pay for it later so in effect you're using someone else's money for that period of time.

Installment payments. Appliances and furniture bought on time from stores are examples. "On time" means either a revolving credit or installment contract. The average APR on both is 18 percent on the first $500 and 12 percent on any additional amount.

If you want to buy something of this sort on time, it's usually more economical to make a loan from your insurance company or bank than to let the store "carry the paper"—jargon for carrying the loan.

Reserve checking. This is offered by some banks as a system of credit along with a checking account. This allows you to write checks for more money than is in your account. If you overspend you won't be charged a penalty. You will have to pay interest, about 12 percent, on the amount you spend over your balance in your account. The amount you may write exceeding your balance is established in advance by yourself and the bank. Actually the coverage is a short-term loan.

Credit cards. Even a credit card is a loan of money. You have lunch, sign a credit card, and repay the money sometime in the future. The total interest rate on credit cards is about the same as the store loans, 18 percent for the first $500 and 12 percent on anything above. If you are slow about paying the credit card bills, the interest winds up costing more than the lunch.

In addition to the cost of using their money, some credit card companies charge an annual fee for the privilege of owning their card. Diner's Club, American Express, and Carte Blanche, are among these.

Most banks that offer credit cards have not been charging an annual fee but many are beginning to. Like the other credit card organizations, banks will charge if the monthly bill isn't paid within a specified amount of time, usually by the end of the next billing period. In the bill a bank may list the total amount due and the minimum amount you may pay. If you pay only the minimum amount, they charge interest on the balance. Interest varies from 10 to 18 percent. Some also charge a late fee if you don't pay even the minimum amount.

MORE ABOUT MAKING A LOAN

When you've shopped and found the best interest rate, you're ready to go in and make your loan. You may feel as nervous as the new girl at school but loan officers on the whole are pleasant people.

I once wanted to make a loan at a downtown bank in Houston and couldn't find a parking place. I double parked, rushed into the bank, called to one of the vice presidents that I needed $1,000 pronto, did he want to lend it to me or not. I didn't have much time. He agreed, signed the proper form, and I was back in the car within five minutes. A few months later I was in Florida where I live in the summer. I wanted a loan again and again I hadn't much time. I began telling the banker of my borrowing experience in Houston. I was getting to the five-minute part when he interrupted. "I can beat their time if you'll just quit talking." And he did.

Possible Difficulties

There's a slight chance you may run into an old-fashioned type who thinks women shouldn't borrow money. This is the official who used to turn women away with a supercilious snarl. He no longer can refuse to lend you money because you're a woman, but he may try.

He may suggest you have inadequate income. He may question your stability. He may say nothing specific but indicate that he is extremely reluctant to lend you money. He is not permitted by law to ask your marital status unless you live in a community property state and your state law makes it necessary. But if he knows you're married, he may suggest you borrow jointly with your husband. He may even ask if your husband knows you want a loan. Don't be swayed by his suggestions. Insist on the loan in your own name.

If he continues to hesitate, try some salesmanship. Think of something that makes you a super good risk. Maybe you want this loan for an investment that is a wonderful opportunity and very, very safe. Tell him about it. Perhaps you can offer some collateral such as an insurance policy or piece of property. If all else fails, and it looks like you're going to be turned down, offer to have a friend co-sign the note. If you do make this offer, make sure in advance that your friend is willing. Co-signing a note means that the co-signer must repay the loan if you don't, so it's not a responsibility to be taken lightly.

If you think he's hesitating simply because you're female, take the offensive. Ask which government agency regulates his organization. Actually an organization's written application form is required to include the name of the federal agency that regulates it. But you want the loan officer to know you're thinking of going to higher authority. You may even say you intend to write a letter of complaint. If your negotiation has reached this point, it may be no help in acquiring the loan but it should make you feel better.

Fill Out the Application

If the loan officer should say there's no point in your applying for the loan because you'll be turned down, insist on filling out an application anyway. Once your application is made, it will be harder to turn you down because the loan officer may have to explain why, and there may be no reason except that you're a woman.

If You're Turned Down

If heaven forbid you're turned down, you're probably going to feel you're a second-class citizen (if not worse), but don't let yourself crawl into an emotional hole. Take positive action. Find out *why* you were turned down. A lender must tell you if you ask. Once you know the objection, set about to correct it.

Then try again.

Probably you won't be turned down. Probably the loan officer will agree to the loan.

Read the Contract

Everyone knows what happens to people who sign contracts without reading them. Everything they own is taken away and they wind up living in a garret. Don't be stampeded by the fact that the loan officer is waiting across the desk, tapping his pencil and eyeing his wristwatch. This is something worth taking time for. Don't just read it, understand it. If there's something you don't understand, ask the loan officer to explain it.

Watch For

1) The way interest is to be computed. You want simple interest, not compound.

2) Clauses charging a penalty if a loan is repaid early. This charge should be modest and compensates the lender only for additional bookkeeping. The penalty is usually on installment loans. On straight term loans most banks don't charge for early payment and many will even rebate your interest to the pay-off date.

3) Wage assignments. This means that the lender can garnishee your wages; that is, ask your employer to send the lender a portion of your salary each month if the loan isn't repaid. This is such a reprehensible clause that you should never allow it to be included in a contract.

Once you've signed the contract, the loan officer presents authorization, you hand it to a teller—and there's your money.

Repay It ASAP

Spend the money as planned. Repay it well before the date required, bearing in mind that your credit rating is on the line. You're only as financially self-reliant as your credit rating, so cherish it well and truly and enjoy your financial independence.

QUIZ

1. Why does a woman need credit?

Because there may come a time when she needs cash and the only

way she can get it is to borrow. Without credit, she cannot borrow
in an emergency. Credit can mean financial survival.

2. If a wife and husband hold all their charge accounts and credit
cards jointly and their credit is good, isn't the wife's credit good without her husband's?

*Legally, yes. The 1975 Credit Act says so. But credit people tradi-
tionally have considered joint accounts the husband's credit only.
The wife in credit terms was a non-person. It's best to take no
chances on your credit status. Make sure you have a good credit
rating in your own name because if an emergency should arise, you
won't have time to establish credit before you need it.*

3. Should a husband and wife close all their joint accounts?

*Not if they like them. But a wife should have at least one bank ac-
count in her own name, and there is little to be said for joint accounts at any time.*

4. How can a woman establish credit?

*Various ways. My favorite is for a woman to open a bank account
in her own name. Use it. After a few months, borrow money from
the same bank. Repay it well before the due date. Once the money
is repaid, she has a good credit rating.*

5. What if the bank won't give her a loan?

*Go to another bank. Most banks will lend money if you have an
account with them and can prove intent and ability to repay.*

6. If a husband dies, can his wife keep their credit cards?

*Yes. But if credit people find out he's dead, they may ask the wife
to reapply in her own name. They then review her credit rating
before reissuing credit.*

7. Are alimony and child support payments considered income?

Yes.

8. Is a bank account in her own name sufficient financial reserve for
a woman? Could she manage in case of emergency?

*She might. But she is well advised to obtain a department store
charge account in her own name and a gasoline credit card if she
owns a car. Then she can manage several months on her own
credit if necessary.*

9.   How can a person find out if she has a credit rating?

Phone the local credit rating agency. They will tell her how to obtain her credit rating if it exists.

10.   If she finds she has bad credit, what can she do about it?

If the bad rating is justified, she can't do anything about it except wait until the report expires, and mend her ways. Negative reports from a collection agency remain on record six years and nine months. If the bad rating is unjustified, she should contact the person or organization that reported erroneously and ask them to set the record straight.

11.   If a woman has credit before she's married, does she keep it after marriage?

Legally, yes. But to make sure her credit isn't blended into her husband's and lost, she should notify her creditors that she is to be married but that she wants to maintain her own credit. If she is taking her husband's name, she should tell them to change the credit to that name but keep it separately from her husband's.

12.   If a woman has a good credit rating and wants to borrow money, where should she go for a loan?

She should investigate lenders in her area to see how much interest they charge. Usually her insurance company, bank, or savings and loan company will have the best interest rate.

13.   If she has bad credit and needs money desperately, should she go to a finance company?

If she does, she'll only wind up deeper in the hole.

14.   How can a person tell how much interest is going to be charged when some contracts are so difficult to understand?

She can ask the creditor to tell her IN WRITING what the Annual Percentage Rate (APR) is. This includes all interest in a contract. He is required by law to tell her the total amount.

15.   What if he doesn't tell her the truth?

She can complain to a government agency, whichever one regulates his business. She has the APR he told her with his signature, concrete evidence of his misdealing.

16. How does she know which agency regulates his business?

The creditor's written application form must include the federal agency that supervises his business. Or she can find out from the local library, the district attorney's office, or the local newspaper.

17. If a single woman wants to buy new furniture, should she put it on her charge account?

The interest rate usually is higher on the charge account than on a loan from a good source. She should check the interest rates and borrow at the lowest one.

18. I found a mistake on my charge account and phoned the store. They said they would correct the mistake but they haven't. What should I do?

WRITE *the store within 60 days after finding the mistake. They are then obligated to clear up the matter.*

19. Can a woman get a home mortgage loan by herself?

Certainly, if she has adequate income. If not, she may be able to find someone to co-sign the loan with her.

20. My mother moved from her home town about 10 years ago and left a savings account at the bank. Will she have trouble getting the money?

If she's done no business with the bank in seven years, they may have closed the account. She can still recover the money but she will have to petition the state. She should write the bank immediately and learn the status of her account.

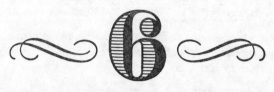

Money, Love, and Marriage

*The Economics of Money When Married
or Living Together*

Wives and husbands need to share financial responsibilities just as they share other day-to-day activities. I don't mean both partners have to contribute income to the family. If one spouse can't or doesn't want to work, that's a personal matter between them. But both should share the responsibility of financial planning and goal setting. Both should share in maintaining expenditures at a reasonable level. The burden of a family's finances is much too heavy for either spouse to bear alone. If two persons are involved, two persons should share responsibilities. If there are children and they're old enough, they, too, should take part in family financial councils. This is a fine training field for youngsters and, handled properly, can prepare them for constructive financial planning when they're on their own.

Almost everything I say applies not only to couples who are married but to those who are living together. Through the remainder of this chapter, I won't draw a distinction between the two except in legal situations.

Ideally a couple should do a great deal of financial planning before they ever marry. Remember you're married not only in the eyes of God but in the eyes of the state. Marriage is among other things a business arrangement. When you marry, you unite two persons into one unit. To make sure that unit is truly cooperative, you need to discuss financial matters before marriage and frequently afterward.

Determine what each of you wants to accomplish financially. Analyze your attitude toward money. Are you a spender or a saver? Occasionally you see two spenders in the same family—total disaster—or two savers, but usually a marriage consists of one each, both struggling to compensate for the other. My aim is to get the two of you together in a happy compromise, some spending in the right places and some saving in the right places, so that in the long run, you'll both be happier.

If you're in any doubt whether you're a spender or saver, answer the following questions. The identification will be obvious.

A. Are you willing to pinch pennies for a few years so you can be more comfortable financially in 15 or 20 years?

B. Or do you prefer to maintain a higher standard of living during early married years with a minimum of improvement financially in the future?

A. Are you willing to work within the confines of a budget?

B. Or do you think a budget would depress and repress you?

A. Are you willing to draw up a plan suited to the needs of your family and adhere to it?

B. Or is it more important to you to live as your friends live even if that varies from your financial needs?

If these questions are answered before you marry, and discrepancies between the two of you worked out to the agreement of both, you should be able to keep financial problems to a minimum. This will give your relationship a much better chance of survival than if you ignore the financial details until you're immersed in them and have to sink or swim. Specifically you should agree on the following:

- A marriage contract, if either of you has holdings or property
- Financial goals
- Agreement on how to reach the goals
- How each salary will be used if both spouses work
- How children, if you plan to have them, will affect the family economy

MARRIAGE CONTRACTS OR PRE-NUPTIAL AGREEMENTS

List in this contract everything you own and stipulate that ownership will remain in your name during your marriage. Upon your death, the properties will pass to the heirs you name. Your husband may wish to do the same with holdings he owns.

This doesn't imply that you don't love or trust your husband. You're simply looking ahead to avoid friction or to fulfill your obligation to other heirs. For instance you may have been married before and have young children. You may want to hold aside funds for their education. Or you may have been widowed and inherited a portfolio of stocks and bonds from your first husband. These belong to you and eventually may pass to your children, if you have any. Your husband may own properties which he wants to bequeath to his children by a previous marriage. This contract is particularly important in a community property state where everything becomes jointly owned legally when persons marry. And it's a good way to avoid misunderstanding in a separate party state.

A pre-nuptial agreement can strengthen your marriage because there's no misunderstanding between the two of you as to what belongs to whom. You don't find two months after marriage that your husband has sold your stock and bought an interest in a gold mine in Peru. Nor will you become involved with his personal holdings unless he requests it. A certain amount of privacy and private ownership can enhance a marriage.

Persons who are living together also should make a list of property belonging to each individual at the beginning of their relationship. Both actor Lee Marvin and rock star Alice Cooper have been sued by girlfriends who claimed the men promised them half their assets. Neither woman had a written contract but one won her case on the basis of an oral agreement.

Don't depend on unwitnessed oral agreements. Who wants to have to sue for what has been promised her? Put it all in writing. That protects both of you.

FINANCIAL GOALS

Few of us would think of starting on a driving vacation without studying a roadmap showing how to reach every major area we plan to visit. Yet how many of us ever think of making a map for our lives? We bumble along, happening upon a job here, a marriage there, a home or two, a child at a fork in the road, a plateau of middle age. If we planned our lives, defined our goals, and worked toward them, we undoubtedly would lead more constructive and personally satisfying lives. Of course we can't foresee everything that's going to happen along the way. We may encounter a detour or a bridge washout. We may even find a shortcut. But the map helps keep us on the right road.

Let's say you're planning to marry, and both you and your husband-to-be are working and plan to continue with your jobs. You might set goals something like this:

ONE YEAR AFTER WEDDING

Establish investment program.
Start looking for home to buy. Will need about $5,000 for down payment.

FIVE YEARS LATER

Time for a baby. Wife will leave work for unspecified period. Decide a year after baby's birth whether to have additional children. Husband's salary must be adequate to maintain family. $15,000? Adjust as necessary.
Maintain investment program.

TWENTY-FIVE YEARS LATER

Child or children educated. Wife returned to work.
Investment program now paying off.
Start making retirement plans.

For another example, let's suppose you've been married 10 years. Your husband earns $12,000 a year after taxes. You have two children, both in elementary school. You're not interested in a career but you've worked off and on during your marriage, never longer than a year at a time. You have a three-bedroom home with a mortgage and one car.

Your family income must be increased because you're unable to put aside money for investment, and expenses for children will increase as they grow older. Your husband can expect salary increases but they won't be sufficient to keep up with needs. Solution: you will find a part-time job.

ONE-YEAR GOAL

Wife will have found part-time work. Family will have rearranged schedules and activities so that each member has certain duties around home to relieve wife of entire responsibility for homemaking. Investment program will have begun.

FIVE-YEAR GOAL

Children are now older and wife will take full-time job.
Investment program continues. If finances are sufficient, family will move to larger home.

TWENTY-YEAR GOAL

Both husband and wife retire when he reaches sixty-five. They sell home and move out of city to small town where they find life more relaxing. Both children have completed their education and are self-supporting. Income from investment program in addition to pensions enables them to live comfortably and take two major trips each year.

These imaginary situations are fairly typical of the way many people live, but they may not fit your expectations of your life. Analyze your own desires. How do you imagine yourself at sixty-five? What do you want to be and do? What do you want to have done?

Identify your long-range expectations. Turn them into firm goals and work steadily toward them.

Division of Salaries

Salaries can be divided in a variety of ways:

1) Both salaries can be combined in one account from which everything is paid.

2) The two salaries and living expenses can be handled separately.

3) The wife can pay for particular items, the husband for others.

Combined salaries: if you combine both salaries, both husband and wife should keep records of monies put into investments. The Internal Revenue Service assumes that the man is the one who pays for investments. If he should die, it is important that you have records proving part of the investments were paid for with your money. You should keep both amounts and dates. Otherwise the value of the investments is counted in the husband's estate and may be taxed.

Separate salaries: if the two salaries are kept separately, make a list of expenses you share, such as rental or mortgage payments, so that each spouse pays an equal share. Of you may prefer to divide it so that the person with the larger salary pays proportionately more. Other expenses you probably would divide would be food, minor household maintenance, utilities, services such as cleaning, property and local taxes, and loans made for the benefit of both of you.

Each person then would pay for her own transportation, clothing, medical bills, insurance, and the like. This involves more bookkeeping but may be worthwhile for other reasons.

Combining and dividing: another way to handle the salaries is for your salary to pay for expenses resulting from your working such as transportation, extra clothing, extra dining out, baby sitting if you have children, with the remainder of the money going into investments. Your husband's salary is used for regular living expenses.

Review Regularly

Review your business affairs at least once a year. Go over everything: income, investments, pensions, insurance. See where you stand financially. Determine where you're going during the coming year. A good time for the review is when you're gathering records to do your income tax.

If you find you're spending too much and investing too little, you may profit from a budget.

MAKING A BUDGET

I've seen budgets drawn up with the care an attorney puts into writing a million-dollar case, done in a fit of organization and a spasm of self-denial. Frequently they follow on the heels of a disastrous occurrence such as a check bouncing or dipping into savings for something nonessential. That sort of budget making is like drawing up a diet after days of gourmet eating or giving up smoking the morning after a party. You're partly ashamed of overspending and partly determined to punish yourself by economizing. There may also be something of the "I'll show you that you can't spend too much and get away with it" attitude from your spouse.

For all these reasons, budgets have a high mortality rate. Most are too restrictive, too tight, too unrealistic. You really cannot feed two persons on $20 a week or four on $30.

A budget is supposed to be your assistant, not your enemy. It works for you, not you for it.

Custom Design a Budget

There are pounds of advice about how to make a budget, what percentage should go for shelter, what percentage to food, etc. Pay no attention to someone else's financial habits. You have your own. The purpose of a budget is not to change your way of living but to help you manage your money. Examine your own habits to see how you should spend and not spend.

In order to make a reasonable, sensible budget

1) Keep track of your expenditures for a couple of weeks. Write down every item and its weekly cost to you; i.e., food, clothing, laundry, rent, transportation . . . everything. When you have completed your two-week total, multiply it by 26. This will give you a good idea of how much you spend day by day for a year.

2) Go through last year's records. List how much you spent in regular items such as rent or house payments, insurance, regular doctor bills such as annual or bi-annual checkups and dentist visits. If you're paying for a car or have another kind of loan that you're repaying at regular intervals, list that.

This is your *hard-core expense list,* the one that you can't do anything about without making major changes in your way of living—like skipping dentist visits and letting your teeth turn to powder.

Hard-core Expense List

HOUSING

Rent/mortgage	$_____
Utilities: gas, elec., water, phone	_____
Other (gardener, cleaning svc.)	_____

TAXES

Property & local	_____
Income taxes (not withheld)	_____

PROTECTION (INSURANCE)

Health	_____
Life	_____
Homeowner's liability	_____
Personal property	_____
Automobile	_____
Other	_____

LOANS (DEBT)

Installment	_____
Charge accounts	_____
Other	_____

PROFESSIONAL EXPENSES

Membership dues	_____
Publications, etc.	_____

MEDICAL AND DENTAL _____

AUTOMOBILE

  Maintenance _____

GIFT TO YOU MONEY _____

OTHER _____

                  TOTAL _____

A necessity, which must be included in your budget, is your *gift to you* money. This is very important and can make the difference between loving or hating your budget. Give yourself a little money from each paycheck. This is yours to have and to hold, or to spend, to do with as you please.

3) Now make a list of irregular but necessary expenditures.

Irregular but Necessary Expenses

Housing maintenance and repair $_____
Car repair   _____
Medical bills   _____
Contributions, religious, other   _____
Gifts, Christmas, wedding, shower, etc.   _____
Other   _____
          Total   _____

4) List the nonessentials that make life a pleasure.

Nonessential Expenses

Clothing $_____
Entertainment   _____
Classes and lessons   _____
Vacation   _____
Furniture   _____
Other   _____
          Total   _____

At this point you have three separate lists from last year's records, plus a list of day-to-day spending.

Combine hard-core expense total with irregular but necessary total with annual total of day-to-day spending.

That total is how much money you must have coming in each year in order to avoid changing your lifestyle or going in debt. Subtract this total from your yearly income. What you have left shows how much you can spend on things which are relatively nonessential such as clothing, entertainment, vacations, classes.

Now—and this is very important—take a portion of this sum out for savings and investment. You must do it even if you wear last year's shoes, spend your vacation at home, and take your classes on educational television. I recommend amounts which vary according to your age and income. If you are young and living on a bare minimum income, then you should take out the bare minimum investment amount, $15 a month. Do this when you first cash your check. Otherwise you'll spend it on something else. Immediately put this sum wherever you've decided to invest. This is a sure way to build your investments.

Once you've subtracted investment money, divide the remainder by 12 so you can see how much you can spend each month on nonessentials. You may find it helpful to set up a Budget Control Sheet similar to the following.

Warning

You've probably decided by now that you're going to have to cut somewhere so you'll have more money in the nonessential, fun list. I hope you can find a way to cut, but don't be unrealistic about car repair, medical bills, or home maintenance. If you don't have a major bill for either one this year, you're likely to be hit doubly hard next year. Or one of the youngsters will step on a rusty nail on a Sunday morning and you'll have to rush to the emergency room of the hospital, which is frightfully expensive, but better than tetanus or gangrene. Part of the reason we have trouble with budgets is in thinking that sort of bill is unusual. Expect unexpected events. Budget for them. Otherwise your whole financial plan will go down the drain.

Overspending

If you or your husband is a consistent overspender, it may help you change your ways if you understand why you're doing it. People overspend for three primary reasons.

1) They don't know how much they're spending in comparison to their income and therefore spend too much.

2) They spend emotionally.

3) They actually lack sufficient income for their needs.

Budget Control Sheet

Expense Category	Budgeted Monthly Average	Month:		Month:			Revised Monthly Average	Month:			Month:		
		Actual	Plus or Minus	Balance Forward	Actual	Plus or Minus		Balance Forward	Actual	Plus or Minus	Balance Forward	Actual	Plus or Minus
Housing													
Food													
Utilities													
Transportation													
Medical													
Life Insurance													
Taxes													
Clothing													
Recreation													
Saving and investment													
Personal improvement													
Church and charity													
Gifts													
Allowance													
Contingency													
Other													
TOTAL													

Know How Much You're Spending

If you draw up the budget plan I've outlined, you'll know where you stand financially. Keep close account of your expenditures and reduce them when necessary and you probably will stay within your budget.

Many people spend too much money because they don't have a clear idea of their financial picture. They buy to gratify immediate needs and worry about balancing the checkbook later.

DANGER AREAS

It is very easy to get into spending trouble with charge accounts. Buy now, pay later is the best policy *if* you always bear in mind that "later" is coming very soon, around the first of the month to be exact.

Too many charge accounts can cause trouble. You charge $25 at one store, $14 at another, $55 at another. None of the purchases is major, but they add up. When the bills come flooding in, you find yourself juggling your available money trying to pay all the charge accounts, already into October's money before September is ended.

TIME PAYMENTS

You can get in debt quickly by buying too much on credit or on time payments. Never commit yourself to a payment schedule that you're going to have trouble meeting. If you want to buy a washing machine that costs $200, and you're going to have to pay $20 per month on it for 10 months, plus another month for interest, make sure you're going to have that $20 available. Some people get themselves into so much trouble with credit buying that they have six creditors chasing them and they're unable to pay any of them.

OVERLOOKING ANNUAL BILLS

Another common reason for overspending is failing to count all necessary expenditures. I've already mentioned the hazards of omitting maintenance and repair bills for home, car, appliances, and medical bills—the unexpected events that you must expect.

Also in this category are the once-a-year bills that are easy to overlook until they come due, such as life insurance, income tax, and state income taxes if you have them. A young divorcée who was having trouble financially came to me for help. She had sufficient income and was careful about unnecessary buying but for the past two years, she had had to borrow money at least once during the year.

We went through her year's receipts and started listing them. Almost immediately we found the culprit. She never thought to include an annual tax which the city levied on property. It was less than $100 but enough to throw her income-outgo picture out of sync. Borrowing money and repaying it at 12 percent interest had added to the problem.

Once we found the leak, she was able to budget accordingly and went on her way rejoicing. She didn't need a money manager. She just needed a little financial detective work.

Discipline. If you lack discipline, start now to be firmer with yourself. I've devised a game which may help when you feel an almost irresistible urge to buy something you really can't afford.

Suppose you see a handbag that is exactly what you need to go with your navy blazer. But it costs $40 more than you should spend for a handbag. Nevertheless you want it desperately.

Take out your checkbook. Write a check for the amount of the handbag payable to your savings account. Turn around. Walk out of the store. Go home, put the check in an envelope, and mail it to your bank. You may find this is an effective way to curb your spending, and the savings account certainly will benefit.

Phobias. If you or your husband overspend in only one particular area, it may be something that's hard to control even if you try very hard to discipline yourself. In these cases you may want to agree that the overspender pay for her excesses with her own money.

A childhood friend of mine develops what is apparently an uncontrollable desire when she is in a certain mood to call friends and relatives whether they're across state, across country, or across the Atlantic. The arrival of the telephone bill signals a day of self-recrimination on her part and indignation on her husband's. Finally they agreed on a solution. Now she pays for the calls with her own money. If she has to do without a new dress, that's her decision.

A man I know consistently succumbs to the lure of tools. He has every variety of screwdriver and wrench known to mankind but he can always find another tool to buy. His wife used to complain that the cupboard was bare but the garage was the best stocked in town. They solved the problem by allotting a set amount each month from his paycheck to buy tools. The wife takes a similar amount from her paycheck to spend on herself.

If you have a problem area, try to work together sensibly to solve it and adjust your budget accordingly.

Impulse Buying

This is a prime money waster. Experts on grocery shopping tell you to go to the store with a list and buy nothing that isn't on the list. The same is true of department stores.

Many people buy clothing they don't need because it's on sale. I have bought beautiful blouses that were such bargains I couldn't resist. They were marked down so much it was like saving money to buy them. Only I had nothing that matched them. By the time I got around to finding something that matched, the blouses were out of style.

Buy "bargains" only if you *need* the item on sale.

Emotional spending. The second major reason for overspending is emotional. When we're unhappy or under more tension than we can handle, we tend to react by overdoing something, eating, drinking, smoking—or overspending. We've been hurt so we give gifts to ourselves. This is all right once in a while but if it happens often, you'll ruin your budget. Better find a less expensive form of compensation.

Inadequate income. After you've figured your hard-core expenses and subtracted them from your yearly income, you may find nothing left. If so, take another look at your fixed expenses.

Rent: Can you save on rent? Can you move to a less expensive home? If you've bought a house, you probably can't do anything about the amount of your mortgage payments, although if you're on a 20-year loan, you could look into changing it to a 25- or 30-year. You'll also have to consider whether your interest rates would increase and the cost of negotiating a new loan, but it's worth investigating. You can probably get all the figures with a couple of phone calls to the organization that holds your mortgage.

Autos: If you own a car, it's probably the second most expensive item in your budget. Maybe you should sell it. You could travel on public transportation or perhaps arrange to ride in carpools for long distances, bicycle and walk for shorter ones.

Food: Can you save on food without sacrificing nutrition? Ground beef and turkey are budget savers. Soft drinks, chips, party crackers, cookies, and the like are money wasters. A few rules for food buying:

- Avoid expensive prepared food such as cakes, pies, delicatessen salads and meats
- Avoid buying in convenience stores where everything is higher

• Watch for sales at nearby grocery stores but buy only if you need the items on sale

Beverages: Soft drinks are expensive, fattening, and bad for your teeth. Beer and liquor are high. If you're teetering on the edge of bankruptcy, don't buy these items.

If you're determined to trim the amount of money you spend, you can almost always do so. But what if you're already in debt?

DEEPLY IN DEBT

Perhaps you've made loans, charged at stores, and bought on time payments until your debts amount to so much that your income can't cover them. You can handle this situation one of four ways.

1) You can take out a new loan, pay off all your creditors and systematically repay the new loan. This may not be the best solution because too many people feel so relieved at having the multitude of creditors off their necks that they start running up new bills.

2) You can go to the creditor to whom you owe the most. Explain your financial problems. Tell him you'll pay your bill on a regular basis and ask his help in reassuring your other creditors that you'll get around to them.

3) You can file a Chapter XIII petition promising to repay part or all of your debts. Chapter XIII refers to a portion of the federal bankruptcy law. In this case a federal judge is in charge. You, your creditors, and a referee plan how you can manage your debts from future income. You either get an extension of time to repay them or occasionally you agree to pay only a certain percentage of what you owe each creditor. Half of your creditors must agree before you can file this petition. Costs of filing, paying the referee, and other expenses can run up to $500, but you do avoid the stigma of total bankruptcy.

4) Voluntary bankruptcy is also a legal step. You list all your assets and liabilities, pay a $50 filing fee, and the court takes over. Your assets are liquidated and the proceeds go to your creditors. Different states allow you to keep different assets, but usually you may retain your clothing and some household goods. Bankruptcy is the worst thing you can have on your credit record and you probably will receive no credit for years to come if you're forced to go this far.

Few people fall this deeply into debt. Usually they trim their expenditures and manage to live within their income. But if you've trimmed to the bone and still lack sufficient money for your needs, perhaps you can think of a way to change the situation.

Increase Your Income

If you're a working woman, you may

1) Improve your skills. Take classes to become more proficient at your work. Even if you have to borrow money to take the classes, it would be worth it.

2) Improve your work performance so you qualify for a salary increase.

3) Take a second job.

If you aren't employed outside the home, you can increase your income by

1) Finding employment outside the home.

2) Finding something you can do in your home for which you'll be paid, such as telephoning, typing, cooking.

3) Make something you can sell.

Before deciding you should go to work, consider how much you can earn and how much you'll have to spend in order to work outside the home. Expenses connected with outside employment include:

- Baby sitting, if you have children
- Transportation
- Extra clothing
- Additional taxes

A young woman I knew wanted to go back to teaching. She enjoyed older children but her two pre-schoolers exhausted her. After figuring all extra costs connected with her work, she found she was clearing less than $200 a month and working about 60 hours a week counting homework. She was earning about $3.00 an hour.

Another woman I knew découpaged wastepaper baskets for her church's bazaar. She became so proficient that she sold them to a department store where they were bought faster than she could make them. Another friend began making dollhouse furniture as a hobby and it became a full-time job which paid her well.

Found Money

Every once in a while, you'll discover some found money. When you've made payments on something for a long time, eventually the payments will end and you'll have found money. You may be tempted to loosen your spending habits and let this additional sum vanish into the who-knows-where, but don't do it. *Invest it.* If you inherit money, or if a child becomes financially independent, take that found money and invest it. Eventually you'll be glad you did.

Overspending is not essential to happiness. Quite the opposite. It causes pains in the stomach and wrinkles in the brow. You may be surprised to find that a neat investment will give you more pleasure than a night on the town, and you won't have a headache the morning after.

POWER OF ATTORNEY

It is wise for wives and husbands to exchange powers of attorney. This is a legal step giving you the right to act for your husband in business and legal matters, and vice versa. I consider this of such importance that my husband's power of attorney was signed on my wedding day and is filed in my safe deposit box along with my marriage certificate.

This document enables you to sign your husband's checks, buy or sell property and stocks, sign contracts, do whatever is necessary to keep business affairs in order. It comes in very handy if your husband should be away on an extended trip or ill for a lengthy period.

You can buy a power of attorney form at an office supply store or you can simply write a letter authorizing a particular person as your agent. State laws vary but you can check them easily at your library or with a local attorney.

CONTRACTS

While we're on the subject of contracts, I want to mention that you should never sign anything without reading and understanding it. I've known many a wife and a husband who sign any contract their spouse puts in front of them, no questions asked. This can be risky even though the spouse has the best intentions in the world. You're liable for debts if you contract them. Your signature on a loan makes you a co-signer. If your spouse doesn't repay, it's up to you to do so. So know what you're signing and if it's a debt, know where the money's coming from to repay it.

Now that we've covered the financial matters connected with connubial bliss, let's make sure the details stick in your mind.

QUIZ

1. I have analyzed my attitude toward money and my husband's attitude and I don't think we'll ever agree. He's a pinch penny. What should I do?

Compromise. If you adopt some of his "pinching" attitude, you may find him loosening the pursestrings somewhat. You may be forcing him to pinch. If you accept as much of the financial planning for your family as he does, you'll be relieving him of a burden —and increasing your own independence and financial responsibility.

2. I have a $10,000 inheritance from my grandmother but if I drew up a pre-nuptial contract, my husband would be hurt. We want to share everything.

Your husband may not be as hurt now as you might be in the future if the money is spent in a way you don't approve. It's difficult to believe before marriage that you could seriously disagree with your loved one about material things, but countless records prove differently.

3. My husband says if we set goals and don't reach them, he'll feel like a failure.

Make your goals realistic enough so that you have a good chance of reaching them. The purpose of goals is primarily to make you identify what you want and plan how to attain it. Your goal is a beacon leading you onward.

4. I went to work so I'd have some extra spending money and not always have to count the cost of everything. Now my husband says it isn't fair that I should buy whatever I like while he pays for the necessities. But he doesn't enjoy buying clothes and knick-knacks. I do. So why shouldn't I be able to if it's my own money?

Again—compromise. What does your husband enjoy buying? Investments, perhaps? If he's paying for all the necessities, perhaps you should divide your salary between the two of you. You buy knick-knacks; he can invest or do with the amount as he chooses.

5. I want to make a budget and I've listed everything as you suggested but my husband won't cooperate. He says he can't keep

track of everything he spends—and frankly, he spends a lot. Can I do it without him?

I guess you'll have to unless he changes his mind. If he refuses to itemize his expenses, ask him to estimate the overall amount he spends. If he won't do even that, perhaps you can figure out the amount by subtracting everything else that's spent from total income. The missing amount should be what he spends. It's hard to budget without cooperation of partners, but you can do it, and I think you're very wise to do so.

6. I can discipline my spending most of the time but I must be a spendaholic. About once a month I go overboard and buy everything in sight. Then my budget is wrecked for another month.

Try the ploy I suggested of writing the check to yourself for the amount of what you would have bought, and mailing it to your savings account. If you wind up short at the end of the month, you can if you must withdraw that amount from savings.

7. It's important for me to dress well and keep my hair done in my work. But I can't do that and save money. Which should I do?

If your work is career oriented, if your appearance will lead to promotions and salary increases, use the money now for your appearance. As soon as the increased money comes through, start saving and investing. If your work is not career oriented, if you have neither opportunity nor desire to improve your position, maybe you should find work where you don't have to spend so much on appearance.

8. I spent a lot on clothes before I was married but my husband and I are very economy-minded so I spend very little now. I'm beginning to look very ordinary and when we go out, I see my husband eyeing the girls who dress better. This doesn't seem fair.

Are you sure it's your husband who's admiring the better dressed girls? Actually it may be you who is admiring them and you're blaming him unjustly. However if your personal appearance really has suffered greatly, perhaps you should put a bit more into it even though your investments are a little less.

9. I couldn't get along without my charge accounts and I never buy anything I don't need, but I spend too much on them. Does that make sense?

Whether or not it makes sense, it happens. You probably buy things you don't need even though when you buy them, you think you need the items. Go through your cosmetics. How many tubes and jars do you have that you haven't touched in months? Go through your linen closets. How many sheets and towels do you have that you never use? How many tablecloths and sets of place-mats do you have that you've never used? Avoid impulse buying. Make a list and buy nothing that isn't on it, regardless of sales and "bargains."

10.   I know delicatessen food is expensive but by the time I get off work, I'm too tired to cook and my husband wouldn't be caught dead in the kitchen.

Try doing your week's cooking on your days off and freezing it in meal-size portions. When you get home from work, you'll only have to heat it, which takes less energy than going to the deli.

11.   Collection agencies call me all the time because I owe so much money here and there. I've considered talking to the people at the store where I owe the most and working things out to pay everybody but that would be so embarrassing.

True. But think of the embarrassment of being dunned and of the energy you're spending worrying about your bills. Talk to your creditors, the sooner the better.

12.   My husband and I don't agree on the best way to invest so he's in the stock market and I'm into real estate. I don't want to give him my power of attorney because he might sell something I didn't want sold. I'm sure he feels the same about his stocks.

When a person signs a power of attorney, he or she agrees to act in your best interests. Your husband would only act for you if you were unable to carry on your business or, if you were on a trip, you could instruct him about measures to take by telephone. If there is some personal reason you haven't mentioned for not giving him your power of attorney, you might prefer to give it to an attor-ney, accountant, or bank trustee so that your business could be carried on as necessary if you were unable to handle it.

For All Women, Single and Married

Financial and legal documents are among your most important possessions. Make a *master list* of important papers and where they're located.

THE MASTER LIST

Begin your master list as you do everything else with name, address, and Social Security number.

List the name of spouse(s), date and place of marriage(s). You don't have to go into a lot of detail here.

List the full names of your children, date and place of birth, current addresses, and guardians if any.

List the Following and Keep Original Documents in Your Safe Deposit Box

- Your birth certificate
- Naturalization papers, if you have any

- Marriage certificates: which may be needed to establish claims for payments from Social Security or other pension plans
- Passport, unless you use it frequently
- Locations of all bank and savings and loan accounts
- If you're divorced or widowed, divorce decree or death certificate
- If you're a military veteran, retirement orders and discharge papers
- Annuities and to whom they are payable
- Real estate holdings and deeds. If there's a mortgage, name the company, amount, and schedule of payments. List property taxes and insurance, and when and where they should be paid
- Car title. If there's a loan, list the amount, when and where it should be paid. Car insurance, when and where due
- Homeowner's insurance policy, when and where due
- Stock and bond certificates if they're not with your broker
- Loan contracts, whether you've borrowed or lent, when due, to whom or from whom
- Government securities if they're not with your broker, when and where due
- Trust documents. List trust officer and his or her address

List and Keep in a Safe Place at Home

- Life insurance policies, names of companies, policy numbers and amounts, and premium payment schedules. Insurance companies have numerous policies which have been paid in full and never collected. The companies make attempts to find heirs if they know of the death of a policy holder, but sometimes they don't even know when a person dies. They have policies worth $5,000, $50,000, occasionally even $100,000 waiting like buried treasure and nobody comes to collect because they don't know about them
- Your will
- Your power of attorney contract
- Federal income-tax returns for the past five years
- Location of your safe deposit box and key

Copy List

Once you've completed the list, make two copies. Keep one at home with your documents, one in a safe deposit box and mail one to your attorney. It is very important to keep these lists in safe places so they don't get lost.

Where to Keep Documents at Home

If you have a safe at home, you can put documents in it. Home safes aren't impervious to professional burglars but they may keep out the amateurs. Don't tell a soul if you do have a safe, not even your best friend, or your children until they've reached the age when they know what to say and not say in public. Not that your best friend would tell a burglar but she may mention it to someone else and a burglar may overhear. If you have a safe, keep it safe by keeping it to yourself.

Some people buy a lockbox. The best ones are supposed to be resistant to fire for several hours, but they're not resistant to thieves. They're small, easy to carry, and look as if they held something worth stealing. I personally prefer something less conspicuous.

Appreciate Your List

Once you've completed your master list, take time to look at it objectively. It's sort of a topographical map of your financial holdings. But like a map of any area under development, your financial map is going to change. You'll buy and sell, pay off debts and contract new ones. As your life progresses, so will your estate. As your estate changes, your master list must be updated.

Try to do it once a year and the logical time is when you're putting together your income-tax return. If you're married, you and your husband should do the updating together, as I said earlier.

Update

Update your will as circumstances demand.

Keep track of your insurance. If you have a whole or straight life policy you may have cash benefits you can use to pay premiums or as collateral for loans. You may even want to borrow the cash itself.

Make sure your homeowners insurance is commensurate with the current value of your home. Property values may have increased so that your home is under-insured. A good real estate agent can give you an idea of how much the home is worth or you can call a real estate appraiser but you'll have to pay him.

Has your passport expired? Renew it now, not when you next decide to leave the country.

Update trusts and annuities as your heirs increase or decrease. Stocks and real estate you owned a year ago may be long gone and replaced. Your business situation may have changed and your pension plans along with it.

Keeping your master list up to date is almost as important as making it in the first place. Besides, it's interesting to see what's happened in the past year. Hopefully you've smoothed out some swampy areas in your financial map, cleared underbrush and built improvements.

When you've finished the updating, make two copies. Send a new one to your attorney and ask him to destroy last year's, put a new one with your record at home and a new one in the safe deposit box.

QUIZ

1.   Should all important papers go into a safe deposit box?

No. A will and life insurance policies should be kept at home so that in case of your death, they would be easy for your heirs to find.

2.   But what happens if the house burns and these documents are lost?

Make copies of them and put them in a safe deposit box. Then they're easily replaced.

3.   What if I've told my heir, my eighteen-year-old son, exactly where all our important papers are but I know he didn't hear a word?

Don't depend on anybody's memory, including your own. Make a master list of all your important papers and their location. Duplicate the list. Put one listing in your safe deposit box, keep one at home, and send the third to your attorney.

4.   If I decide to sell my house and buy a condominium, the master list would be inaccurate.

Update it regularly, at least once a year. Also update trusts and annuities.

5.   Is it really important to update a master list as often as once a year?

Yes, if you've made any changes in properties or have increased or decreased heirs.

6.   I think my home has increased in value but I don't want to pay a fee to an appraiser just to satisfy my curiosity. Is appraisal by a realtor reliable?

Often appraisers call real estate companies to find out how much homes are selling for in particular areas. Unless you're actually planning to sell your home, a real estate appraisal is as accurate as an appraiser's and a lot cheaper. However an appraiser is more likely to spot structural damage, such as a broken foundation, which would lower the value of your home until the damage was repaired.

Woman on Her Own

Special Tips for the Widow and Divorcée

A wife's chances of becoming single are unfortunately very great. If you don't divorce, you probably will outlive your husband. It's an unpleasant prospect and all of us would rather think about something else, but the primary reason most widows and divorcées have such difficult times financially is because they've never faced this possibility.

Women generally live longer than men. Statistics show the number of divorces is increasing steadily. You may be one of the lucky ones who never has to become single after being married. I hope you are. But you are very wise to plan as if someday you would have to get along without your husband. Hope for the best; plan for the worst.

I've known many widows, divorcées, and wives whose husbands simply disappeared. I've advised many of them and I've helped them pick up the pieces of their lives and fit them into a new mold. And I've come to one conclusion.

The best way to protect yourself financially is to be able to support yourself, to be aware of financial matters in your marriage, and to own some properties if at all possible in your name alone.

There are some things you can do, as I've mentioned in other places in this book, to help yourself financially if you're suddenly widowed. There are steps you can take if divorce is up-coming. But the best protection of all is to be able to take care of yourself and own something of value.

Let's review the steps every woman should take for her own financial protection.

If you're not married but planning to be

1) Maintain your credit when you marry.

2) If you have holdings, make a pre-nuptial agreement that keeps them separate from joint ownership.

If you're already married

1) Develop a credit rating by opening your own bank account, making a loan after a few months, repaying it early.

2) Open a charge account at a major department store.

3) If you drive a car, obtain a gas credit card.

4) Keep enough money in your own bank account to see you through several months' expenses.

5) Own your husband's insurance policy.

6) Make sure your husband has made a will. This is discussed later at length. Husbands need to prescribe in a will how their estates will be distributed. Don't simply assume that you will inherit everything if your husband dies without a will.

If you take these steps, you'll be able to manage financially for several months if you're faced with an emergency.

But eventually the emergency period will pass. You'll redevelop a normal life. This is the time when your knowledge of money management and ability to support yourself becomes important.

Abandonment can cause more problems financially than widowhood and divorce because property ownership is in a state of limbo. Emotionally, however, widowhood probably is hardest.

IF YOU ARE WIDOWED

1) Don't take any major steps if you can avoid them for a year after your husband's death. Your emotional condition is likely to keep you from thinking rationally enough to sell your home or dispose of other valuable holdings. You need a period to mourn and to decide how to carry on your life.

2) If your husband has a lengthy illness before death, make sure you take all deductions allowed on your income tax. These vary

somewhat from year to year, but your attorney or accountant can tell you what is deductible at the time.

3) Find out from your attorney or accountant whether the estate will have to go through probate. State laws vary on this point. If probate is necessary, your husband's debts will be paid during this process and assets distributed according to his will.

4) If your husband had debts, he may have taken out insurance to cover them. Examine insurance papers to determine this.

5) If your husband died as a result of an accident, do any of his insurance policies pay extra benefits?

6) Do any of his health policies include death benefits?

7) Go over all insurance policies carefully with your insurance agent to make sure you're not overlooking any benefits.

8) Do likewise with pensions—company, private, military.

9) Talk with officials at the Social Security office to see if you and/or your children qualify for payments. Children under eighteen and students under twenty-two probably qualify. So probably do you if you're over sixty, or younger if you're partially or totally disabled.

10) Go over any annuities and trust funds with your attorney but, as I said before, avoid making important decisions for a year or so, if you can.

11) If you and your husband have a joint safe deposit box, you may save bother by removing everything from it before the bank knows of his death. If he is ill prior to death, you can empty the box before his demise.

12) Destroy your husband's credit cards, unless you want to use them.

13) If you're working outside the home, maintain your job. If you're not, you may want to find a job. This gives you both income and an outside interest.

14) If your estate is of any size and you want to pass it on to heirs, talk with your attorney how best to go about this. Taxes are heavy when a single person dies, but you may be able to take certain steps to make them lighter.

Most of these steps have to be taken after your husband's death. The opposite is true for a divorcée. She needs to take protective steps before the split.

IF YOU ANTICIPATE DIVORCE

If you think divorce is unavoidable, it may help to know some facts about divorce itself, decisions you need to make, and steps you need to take.

Divorce laws vary greatly so it is important to check laws in your own state to determine fine details. Most public libraries have copies of their state divorce laws. Phone to make sure your library has the law. If not, they can tell you where to find it.

There are major differences in the divorce laws of community property and separate property states. In the community property states (Arizona, California, Idaho, Louisiana, Nevada, New Mexico, Texas, and Washington), all properties accumulated during your marriage are assumed to belong to both of you. Properties owned prior to marriage usually are assumed to belong to the original owner. The division between spouses usually is fairly even although if you have children, the person who keeps them may receive more of the property, perhaps 60 percent.

Separate property states assume for the most part that properties accumulated during the marriage belong to your husband. Efforts have been made in many states to assess the monetary value of a homemaker's contribution to the marriage, but it is still likely to be discounted when the property is counted and distributed. Some states and some judges make an effort to divide property fairly evenly between spouses; others don't.

I said earlier it is important to keep records if your money has helped purchase investments because of capital gains tax. The inequality of divorce procedures is a second excellent reason for keeping good records—you can prove part of the properties are yours.

Warning

If you think a divorce is likely and your husband suddenly wants to move to a different state, check divorce laws in that state. This happened to a woman I knew. She moved from a state with good alimony and child-support laws to one where there was next to no financial protection for a divorced wife and children. In reviewing the couple of years preceding the divorce—which he insisted upon—she came to the conclusion that he had moved for the express purpose of saving himself money at her expense. To this day he's never paid a dime of alimony or child support. He wouldn't even help pay for their daughter's wedding.

Try to Work Out Details with Your Husband

Divorce is expensive both emotionally and financially. If you've been married for any length of time and have children, both you and your husband probably will have to change your life style.

The divorce itself can cost from between a few hundred to several thousand dollars depending upon the size of your estate and the amount of time your attorneys have to spend settling details. The best way to save legal fees is for you and your husband to work out details between you before the attorneys ever come into the picture.

Decide the following:

1) If you have children, who gets custody of them? If you keep the children, how much child support will their father pay? Child support normally continues until a child reaches eighteen, gets a full-time job, or marries. When and how often will your husband have the children? What extras such as special classes, trips, and equipment will he pay for?

2) How the property is going to be divided

3) Specifically who gets what

4) If you live in a separate property state, do you want your share in a lump sum or alimony (community property states don't award alimony)?

Lump Sum or Alimony?

The lump sum has advantages: you have it in hand, and you don't have to pay tax on it.

It also has disadvantages: you may be tempted to live on it instead of investing it so that it will be building capital for you; if your husband's salary and assets increase, you have no opportunity to receive an additional portion.

If alimony is awarded, combined with child support it usually amounts to 30 to 50 percent of a husband's salary. The actual amount depends both on the court's decision and on your age and abilities. If you're over forty and unlikely to find a good job, you may be awarded more than if you're younger and capable of making your own living.

The advantages of alimony are that you may be able to include an escalation clause in your settlement or petition the court so that your alimony increases along with your former husband's salary.

Its disadvantages:

1) Your husband may not make the alimony payments in spite of what the court decreed.

2) You have to pay tax on alimony because it is income.

3) If you remarry, alimony stops.

4) If you work and make a good salary, the alimony can be reduced.

Another possibility is an alimony trust, and there are two kinds. One is a trust originally set up as a marital trust but can be converted to an alimony trust. You don't pay tax on this kind. The second kind is one established specifically to pay alimony. On this, you do pay income tax.

Alimony trust advantages:

1) You have a sure source of income—much more reliable than alimony.

2) You have no assets to invest and no large lump sum to manage.

3) This may appeal to your former husband if he's in a high tax bracket because he can reduce his taxable income but eventually get back the trust principal or make it part of his estate.

The only disadvantage to an alimony trust is that it takes a good sized income to make an alimony trust a consideration.

Things to Beware Of

If you and your husband try to work out a settlement before calling in attorneys:

1) Avoid listing assets to be divided. Simply state that property will be divided evenly or whatever you decide on. If you start listing assets and their value, you're likely to overlook something important.

2) Don't get involved at this time with sentimental objects such as photographs, family heirlooms, favorite books and paintings. These can bog down the talks indefinitely. Settle everything else and both of you sign agreements before venturing onto this emotional ground. Divorce lawyers have told me of proceedings being held up for months over ownership of phonograph records and the like.

3) Division of property is likely to involve capital gains taxes if you're dividing properties such as homes, real estate, or stocks and bonds that have appreciated during your marriage. When you transfer ownership from one person to another, or change from joint ownership to single ownership, you have to pay tax on the appreciated value of the property. This is another good reason to avoid joint ownership and to own properties in your own name. If they're already yours, there's no question of transferring ownership. If it's too late for you to do this, talk to your attorney about how best to avoid high taxation on property division.

Note to parents: If you're buying property for an adult child who's married, make it a personal loan instead of an outright gift. If the marriage should break up, the property then will revert to you legally and can be retained or sold by your child.

WHAT YOU SHOULD RECEIVE AS PART OF YOUR SETTLEMENT

1) Your husband's life insurance policy. If you're going to be very short of money, he may agree to continue paying premiums.

2) If you have children, you may want to keep your home. This provides the children with familiar surroundings and a sense of continuity in spite of other changes in their lives. As part of the settlement, your husband may continue home payments or even pay off the mortgage.

3) If the mortgage is paid off, will your husband pay for homeowners insurance?

4) If you've been carried on your husband's health and disability insurance policies, you'll have to get new policies. Will your husband pay for them? Any children definitely should remain on his policies.

5) If your husband pays child support, he also will claim the children as dependents. If you plan to work, it would be advantageous for you to claim one child as a dependent so that you can take child-care deductions. This can save you several thousand dollars a year.

6) Who will pay attorneys' fees? Usually a husband pays these fees because usually his income is higher.

7) Do you have club memberships you want to maintain? Your husband may continue to pay annual assessments, especially if your children use facilities such as tennis courts and swimming pools. Is the waiting list for your club so long that if you have to give up membership, you won't be able to rejoin?

It may be difficult to work with your husband to settle these points. Both of you are likely to feel hurt, anger, and guilt—all destructive emotions likely to cause either of you to explode over the slightest disagreement. Try to carry on the negotiations as you would any other business matter. Try to put emotions aside until agreement is reached.

HIRE AN ATTORNEY

Charges probably will depend on the amount of property to be divided. Call the local bar association and ask if they have recommendations on fees to be charged for divorces. Suppose you and your husband have an annual income of $25,000. Ask what the recommended fee is for a divorce involving that amount of income. Then look for an attorney who agrees to charge about that amount.

When you find one, get a written statement saying he or she will charge that amount, except in the event of unforeseen hazards such as a breaking of the agreements between you and your husband.

You want the attorney to do two things: (1) to go over the agreements you've made with your husband to make sure you haven't missed anything, and (2) to file a petition for divorce.

Don't

1) Don't pick a lawyer with little experience in divorce law. You want somebody who knows what he or she is doing.

2) Don't believe a lawyer who tells you he can get you a great settlement. Ultimately the settlement will be decided by the court, and you can tell about what kind of settlement you can expect by checking what's happened in the past couple of years in your area.

DO-IT-YOURSELF DIVORCE

If you have very little property to divide, you may be able to dispense with an attorney and go directly to court. This was possible at this writing in three states: California, New York, and Washington. Divorces under $35 are possible in Texas.

FAULT–NO-FAULT

There are two kinds of divorce, commonly described as fault and no-fault. Fault divorces ascribe most of the blame to one person. These are the ones we're familiar with from newspaper stories.

In order to be awarded the divorce, one person has to prove the other has committed acts heinous enough to end the marriage. These can become very expensive if the divorce is contested by the spouse being sued. For instance, if you sued your husband charging him with adultery and he counter-sued charging you with cruelty, you could be into a very messy situation. You run the risk of unpleasant personal matters being aired in court, an embarrassment to both of you. If children are involved, these revelations can be even more destructive. Attorneys have to spend more time, so fees mount. About the only time these divorces are worthwhile is when you have led a blameless life and your husband has committed grievous faults. The court is more likely to be sympathetic to you and award a good settlement.

No-fault divorce eliminates recriminations and allows you to terminate a marriage on the grounds of irreconcilable differences which have caused the irretrievable breakdown of the marriage. This simplifies legal proceedings, which is desirable, but may provide you a lesser settlement. The division of property then is based on the relative economic circumstances of you and your husband.

Other grounds for no-fault divorce are incurable insanity, living apart for a given period of time, and incompatibility.

States that allow no-fault divorce are Arizona, California, Colorado, Florida, Hawaii, Iowa, Kentucky, Michigan, Missouri, Nebraska, Oregon, and Washington.

States that recognize both fault and no-fault are Alabama, Alaska, Delaware, Idaho, Indiana, Kansas, Maine, Nevada, New Hampshire, New Mexico, North Dakota, Oklahoma, Texas, and Wyoming.

A few states also recognize alimony for husbands.

Alimony For Him

If you're the larger income earner in your marriage, your husband may be awarded alimony in a few states. A California woman told me of her financial difficulties since her divorce. I asked if her former husband made any contribution to her income. "Hah!" she snorted. "I was lucky not to have to pay him alimony." There has also been a case where a husband who kept his child sued his former wife and was awarded child support.

Residency Requirements

You have to live in most states one year before you can get a divorce, although some states require residency of only three or six months. Nevada and Idaho require only six weeks'. residency.

If you're in a hurry for a divorce, you may want to go to one of these states. If your spouse is notified and doesn't contest the action, you're awarded a divorce by default. You cannot, however, get child custody and support, alimony, or property division. These can be settled only in the state where your former husband resides. Sometimes spouses later contest divorces granted in these two states on the grounds that residency was not established. To make sure such a divorce is legal, you should behave as if you planned to live in the state awhile. Lease a home, register to vote, do anything else you can think of which indicates intentions of long-term residency.

YOUR RIGHTS AS A DIVORCÉE

Normally a creditor can't close an account because you change marital status unless he has evidence that you're unwilling or unable to pay.

A creditor may count alimony and child support as part of your income. He is also required to tell you that unless you rely on alimony or child support for income to obtain credit, you don't have to disclose that income.

If your husband neglects paying child support, your state may have agencies that will seek him out through Social Security payments and other official records. Again your research librarian can tell you if your state has such an agency and how to contact it.

Now let's see how much you remember.

QUIZ

1. What are the best ways to protect yourself financially against the possibility of widowhood or divorce?

   Be able to earn your own living; be aware of financial activities in your marriage; if possible own some property in your own name.

2. If widowed, I think I'd sell my home immediately so I wouldn't be reminded of my husband everywhere I looked.

   It's wiser to make no major decisions for at least a year after being widowed. Emotional upset may keep you from thinking rationally for some time.

3. My husband has four life insurance policies and a private health plan. I don't understand some of the provisions. How would I know if I was overlooking some benefit in case of his death?

   Go over the policies either with agents from the different companies or with your attorney to make sure you receive all benefits due.

4. My husband and I have joint credit cards. Can I keep using them after his death?

   If the credit card company doesn't know he is dead, yes. But it's safer to have cards in your own name.

5. How can I find out exactly what the divorce laws are in my state?

Call the public library. They should have copies of the divorce laws on file. If they don't, they can tell you where to find them.

6. How much does a divorce cost?

That depends on how much property you and your husband have, and how much time an attorney has to spend on your case.

7. My husband said, "Sure, get a divorce. I'll go along with whatever you want." But he won't discuss how we're to divide our assets. What should I do?

Write an agreement saying the two of you will divide assets evenly and both of you sign it. If you have children whom you will take custody of, divide property about 60–40 in your favor.

8. I think it would be safer to take my settlement in the form of a lump sum, but I'm not sure what to do with it. If I put it in the bank, I'll spend it.

If you're unfamiliar with investments, study the investment chapter in this book. Pick a safe investment, such as CD's, and deposit the lump sum. After further study, you can decide on a permanent investment program.

9. My husband went into his own business last year. He's not making much yet but prospects look very good for the future. I've worked and helped him so I think I deserve a share of the future rewards, but if I get a divorce this year, the settlement will be low because company income is still low.

Ask for an escalation clause in your alimony agreement saying that your alimony will increase along with your former husband's income, if you live in a separate property state. If you live in a community property state, ask your attorney how you can benefit from future company profits.

10. I received a high alimony and child-support settlement but then my husband moved to another state and won't pay anything.

Perhaps if your settlement had been lower, your husband wouldn't have moved. Find out from the library if your state has an agency which will trace former husbands who refuse to pay their obligations. If so, they may be able to help you.

Your Own Money

The Dynamics of Being Single

The woman on her own has the same problems with money that the married woman has—how to get it and how to keep it. The difference for the woman who has not married is that the getting it is entirely up to her and that what she keeps is all her own to do with as she pleases. The single who has been married may have either an inheritance or settlement with which to begin her new life. She also may have children whom she supports fully or partially. But basically the problems are the same.

How are you going to get it?

How are you going to keep it?

What do you ultimately want to do with it?

The woman on her own has many financial advantages. She's free to make her own choices about how to handle her money. If she needs to economize, she probably can do so more easily than the married. She can save on food—a high expense in any budget—without sacrificing nutrition with meals that husbands and children probably would not eat. The time spent by a married woman on her family can be put by the single into such things as overtime to make more money or improve a job position, study to improve a work or investment program, entertaining to advance a career, sewing to save money on clothes, and so on.

There are disadvantages too, especially if you're a single who has been married, and accustomed to depending upon your husband for consultation and advice on financial matters. It may take a while for you to trust your own financial judgment but if you persevere, the time will come, perhaps sooner than you think, when you find that you do feel confident about your money and the way you're handling it. And the satisfaction of doing it on your own is very great.

Now let's think about your life plan. Just as you need a set of blueprints before you build a house, so you need a plan in the construction of your future life. The broad outline of your personal blueprint will be formed by basic needs. These include:

1) *Living expenses* should come from your salary, alimony, dividends from stocks, etc. Any lump sum you receive should be invested —not spent on living costs.

2) The amount of *emergency funds* you need depends on your age, health, and personal feelings about security. Determine how many months' income you need readily available to make you feel secure. Keep that amount in secure savings. Certificates of Deposit are as safe and as available as savings accounts, and they normally earn more interest.

3) *Health insurance* may be available to you in a group plan where you work. Compare the group plan to a private one. Consider which offers better coverage and which costs more and how likely you are to stay at the company where you now work. If you go to another job or if your job should be terminated when you are fifty-five, what would you do about health insurance? You may be wise to buy your own policy while you're young, healthy and very insurable.

4) Everything I said about health insurance applies also to *disability insurance*. For more details, review that subject in the chapter on insurance.

5) *Income when you no longer earn a salary* must come from investments, pensions, and private company plans such as profit sharing. Study any company pension plans thoroughly before taking part in them if you have a choice. If you change jobs, you could lose your pension. If your job is terminated, you might lose pension benefits. Again you may be better off in the long run to open your own IRA fund. This doesn't stop along with your job.

6) You can keep *life insurance* to a minimum if you have no de-

pendents. A policy for $10,000 should be adequate. If you need protection for dependents, you'll need more life insurance.

Those are the basic needs which must be provided for whether you're twenty or sixty. Now let's be more specific.

Suppose you're twenty-five with no dependents. You have a job that pays an adequate salary and offers fairly good chances for promotion. You have almost $2,000 in savings. You have group health insurance at your company but you're not sure what it covers. You're fairly certain it doesn't include disability. When you've been with the company three more years, you can take part in their profit sharing plan. You have no investments.

One-year goal: you want at least one promotion and salary increase within a year. You've studied the group health policy and compared it to a private plan. You've clarified the disability situation and taken out insurance if you have none on the group plan. You've also studied the company's profit-sharing plan and compared it with other pensions. You've put most of your savings into Certificates of Deposit. You're seriously studying different ways of investing.

Five years from now: you have a higher salary and better position either with your present company or another one. You've bought a home and car. You're taking part in a good, reliable pension plan, and hope to start within the next two years on an investment program. You've bought a term life insurance policy.

Twenty years from now: you want to be earning a good income either with a company or in your own business. Your pension plan is still in effect. Your investments are paying dividends. You've converted your term insurance to an inexpensive whole life policy. You've maintained your health and disability insurance.

Plans look good for a financially trouble-free future.

For another example, let's say you're thirty-five, divorced, and have two children of elementary school age. You're going back to office work. You have a small settlement from your former husband of $3,500, half the assets the two of you had accrued in ten years of marriage. Your husband has promised to pay child support of $100 a month. You're still in the family home but don't think you want to keep it. You have no insurance, no investments, no pensions.

One-year goal: you've found employment, sold your former home and bought a smaller home or rented an apartment near your office. You've moved the children to another school, arranged carpools for them and found a sitter who stays with them after school. You've taken out private health and disability insurance, and a minimum life policy (your former husband's policies name the children as beneficiaries, and his health policy covers them). You have less than $1,000 in savings because your settlement and your share of the house sale went into buying the townhouse. You realize you must make more money in order to start investment and pension programs.

Five-year goal: you enrolled in one night class each semester to improve your job qualifications and your employer has sent you to two special week-long schools. You've received promotions and salary increases within the company so that your income now enables you to invest. You've opened an IRA fund, studied investments, and have just borrowed $3,000 to make a real estate investment.

Twenty-five-year goal: you're now sixty. Your company was bought ten years ago by a larger one and your job was phased out. However your job qualifications and record were so good that you easily found employment in spite of being over fifty.

Your investments are about evenly divided between real estate and the stock market. Your IRA fund has grown. You have become interested in antiques and spend time shopping and renovating furniture. Your investments and pension will enable you to retire in five years if you choose, although retirement is not mandatory.

Suppose you're forty-five and newly widowed. You have a child in college and one in high school. You inherited half your husband's estate, $21,000. The other half was divided evenly between the children. You have a home with eight years of mortgage payments left and a car.

Your husband had no private pension plan and you will receive no Social Security payments until you're sixty. You have no life insurance, health or disability insurance. Your husband had a few stocks, but you haven't kept track of their performance. You haven't worked in fifteen years but have been thinking about selling real estate.

One-year goal: decide what you want to do to earn income and take any training necessary. Purchase health and disability insurance, and a small life policy. Examine stocks and decide whether to keep them. Put the $21,000 in savings and decide where to invest it permanently.

Five-year goal: to be actively pursuing a career, probably real estate. Have an active investment program. Probably will have moved to smaller home.

Twenty-year goal: investment program provides sufficient income to live on. Continue to pursue career while at the same time enjoying more leisure time.

You see the importance in all these examples of making plans and moving steadily toward financial independence. Suppose the forty-five-year-old woman had left her $21,000 in a savings account. She could never have depended upon it to do more than see her through an emergency. She had to inform herself on investments and place it in a position where it could grow.

BUYING A HOME

One of the best investments you can make is to buy a home because a home is a necessity and because buying is cheaper than renting.

The kind of home you choose will depend upon your

- income
- geographical location (city, town, country)
- personal preferences

Income: I'll go into this in depth later. For the moment, I'm simply mentioning, as if you didn't know, that it is one of the major considerations in your choice of a home.

Location: the community in which you live probably will make about as much difference in the type of home you choose as income. In New York City and Chicago, if you live inside the city, you'll probably find it simpler to live in an apartment or condominium than in a house.

At the other end of the spectrum, in the country or in a small town, you may be forced to live in a house. Apartments are limited in small communities and townhouses almost nonexistent. You may find a duplex or occasionally that near-anachronism, a garage apartment. At least one old house probably will have been turned into a boarding house.

Mobile homes are to smaller towns what apartments are to big cities. If a town is so small it doesn't have a mobile home park, a mobile home can be put on a rented lot.

Personal preferences: being human beings packed with emotions, our personal preferences about dwellings have to be considered. Some people prefer to rent. Others aren't happy unless they own their home. Some feel incomplete without a yard. Others like the feel of a high-rise apartment. Analyze your own preferences and decide what kind of dwelling you would prefer.

Let's consider the kinds of home from which you may choose, their advantages and disadvantages.

HOME	ADVANTAGES	DISADVANTAGES
Boarding House	inexpensive location* mobility low maintenance	lack of privacy lack of space location*
Apartment	good location relative mobility low maintenance	lack of privacy space limited no tax advantage no investment qualities
Co-op Apartment	good location low maintenance tax advantage investment possibilities	lack of privacy space limited
Mobile Home	relatively inexpensive relatively mobile tax advantage	space limited rapid value deterioration neighborhoods limited requires maintenance hard to finance appearance outside†
Townhouse	location low maintenance relatively low cost tax advantage good investment	lack of privacy space limited
House	good investment tax advantage yard neighborhood	cost location high maintenance

* Location can be both a plus and minus. Usually boarding houses are close to the center of town, which is convenient. Frequently they're in a deteriorating part of town, which is undesirable.

† That's a value judgment. Some people think mobile homes are lovely outside. I think they're much more attractive inside.

As you can see, many of the items listed as advantages or disadvantages are relative. For instance I say the space is limited in a condominium. That depends on your basis for comparison. Compared to a house, usually the space is more limited in a condominium. Compared to a boarding house, it is spacious. There is quite a bit of privacy in a condominium or expensive co-op apartment too, although less than in a single-family dwelling.

I also list neighborhood as an advantage for a house. A neighborhood can of course be pleasant or unpleasant. I'm assuming that if you buy a house, you'll buy it in a neighborhood pleasing to you.

When choosing a home you must consider three primary features: (1) maintenance, (2) location within the community, and (3) cost.

The other considerations such as space, privacy, and mobility can be adjusted to. But the big three need to be considered carefully before you make a firm choice.

Maintenance: If the thought of tending a yard or replacing roofs or repainting outside walls boggles your mind, you'd probably better stay away from a house. A condominium or townhouse requires less heavy maintenance.

Location: This may be as important as the home itself. You'll want to be close to work, school, church. You'll want to be in a safe neighborhood. If you have children, you'll want to consider which schools they'll attend and how they'll get there.

Cost: It's cheaper in the long run to buy than to rent. I'll explain why later. But the initial expense is a big consideration.

Immediate costs when buying:

- down payment
- homeowners insurance
- moving charges
- closing costs
- attorney fees
- utility deposits*
- furnishings (draperies, appliances, etc.)†

In addition to immediate costs, you have
Additional costs during the first year:

- property taxes
- maintenance and repair‡

* If you've paid your own utilities in the city where you buy, you may not have to make deposits.

† You may be able to buy a home which requires no additional furnishings.

‡ If you buy a townhouse or condominium, you probably will have no maintenance outlay during the first year but you probably will pay a maintenance fee. If you buy a new house, you probably also will avoid maintenance charges the first year. If you buy an older house, you probably will have bills the first year.

- school taxes
- transportation*

Too often persons plan to spend about the same on mortgage payments as they did on rent. It's easy to overlook those other bills they're going to have that most renters don't worry about, such as utilities. Few renters pay directly for their utilities although an increasing number of apartments are requiring tenants to pay their own.

ESTIMATE ALL EXPENSES

The first thing to do if you're thinking about buying is make a list of projected expenses. Leave out the mortgage itself for now.

Homeowners Insurance. Prices vary greatly among states and insurance companies. To get an estimate of cost in your locality, ask a reliable realtor, mortgage company, bank, savings and loan company, or go directly to an insurance agency.

Property and School Taxes. These taxes can vary greatly so check in your own area. The same sources who told you about insurance can tell you about property and school taxes. So can the tax assessor's office at city hall.

Utilities. Prices are soaring with predictions that within a few years, utilities will cost as much as mortgage payments. Ask a realtor to give you an estimate of what utilities run in your area. If you want to be more specific, check with the individual companies. You'll have electricity, water, garbage, and whatever fuel is used. You also have telephone, although that charge is the same in an apartment unless you add an extension in your home. If you've never paid utilities before, the electric company may require a deposit of around $50 before they agree to extend service. In a year or two they should refund the deposit. If they don't, ask them to.

Furnishings and Appliances. You may have to buy a few other things. If you're leaving an apartment, you may have to buy a refrigerator, washer, dryer, or other expensive items. Little things include shower curtains, garbage cans.

You may have to put up curtains, shades, or draperies in your new home. You can live without a lot of things but window coverings are not one of them. If you buy a new house, you'll have all the windows to cover. Builders normally put in carpeting but not window coverings. If you buy an older house, the previous owner may leave draperies or shutters. Even if they don't match your furniture, they're

---

* You may have additional transportation charges when you buy a new home.

great to have at first when you're spending so much in other ways.

Condominiums and co-op apartments usually include window as well as floor coverings.

If you buy a house, you'll also have a yard. New house, new yard, and some expense is involved even if you plant it yourself. You'll probably want a fence if you have small children or a dog. More expense.

You can avoid the yard if you buy a townhouse or condominium, but you pay a maintenance fee.

After you've put together all the costs, add them up. Costs for a $30,000 home might run something like this. This is very iffy, but it will give you some idea.

			YEAR	MONTH
Taxes			$600	$50
Homeowners insurance			300	25
Maintenance (average over				
30 years)		house	300	25
	or	condominium	120	10
Utilities			1200	100
	Totals	house	$2400	$200
		condominium	$2120	$175

Now add your current expenses excluding rent. Combine that figure with your projected expenses. Suppose your expenses total $600 a month. Add that to the estimated costs of owning a home.

Current expenses	$600
Estimated future expenses	$200
	$800

Subtract that total from your monthly income after taxes.

Suppose you make	$1100
	− 800
	$ 300

That leaves you $300 for monthly mortgage payments.

You also must consider the one-time expenses necessary when you buy. The largest will be the

Down payment: This varies with the price of the home you buy, the kind of loan you make, and your age. Older people can rarely get a 30-year loan. If you qualify for a GI loan, you can have a lower down payment than a standard mortgage loan. Usually the higher priced a home is, the more you have to pay down. Loan companies want to make sure, if they're lending you a hundred thousand for a luxury condominium, that you're in good shape to repay it, so they may ask as much as a third down. If you're buying a $30,000 home you may be able to make a down payment of only about 10 percent or $3,000.

Other one-time expenses include:

- moving
- furnishings
- utility deposits
- attorney's fee

So far the financial picture has been all out and nothing in. So now let's talk about the advantages of buying.

Advantages of Buying

As I said earlier, it's cheaper in the long run to buy than rent. When buying you have

1) A tax advantage or shelter. You write off your loan interest and all property and school taxes on your income tax.

2) An investment. Should you sell your house at projected inflation prices, you will likely make a profit. A recent national survey showed that 80 percent of home buyers do so with the thought that a home is a good investment.

Tax Advantage. You deduct the interest on the mortgage loan. This amounts to more the first few years of the loan than later because the first few years of payments apply primarily toward interest charges. Only a little bit applies to the loan principal. You're not really paying for the home yet. You're paying for the use of the money you borrowed to pay for the home, As time goes on, more and more of the money applies to the principal. Eventually most of the payment goes to principal and only a small amount to interest.

You can also deduct the property and school taxes from income tax. Otherwise you'd be paying tax twice on the same money.

Using those same hypothetical figures used earlier, your financial situation relating to your home looks something like this. You bought a $30,000 home with a $5,000 down payment. Principal and interest, also known as the mortgage payment, run about $2,200 a year on a 30-year loan. We estimated insurance, maintenance, and utilities at $1,800 a year. Taxes at $600 a year brought the figure up to $2,400. Add $2,400 to the mortgage payment of $2,200, and the total annual cost is $4,600.

Of this let's say $1,800 is interest the first year on the loan. You deduct the $1,800. You also deduct property tax which we estimated at $600. That makes a total deduction of $2,400.

Subtract the $2,400 from $4,600. You get $2,200 which you are spending each year on your home, slightly more than $183 per month. You probably paid more than that in an apartment with no hope of getting a penny back.

Let's say you want to buy and you have adequate income. You've decided what part of town you prefer so location is determined. You've decided how involved with maintenance you want to be. In other words, you know whether you want to buy a condominium, townhouse, or house. Following are some things to watch for.

CONDOMINIUM

Maintenance Fee: Find out how much it is. Some fees are very expensive. Or you may find one which purports to have no maintenance fee at all. Check that out very carefully. Somebody's got to pay for taking care of things and it's not likely the developer's planning to do it out of his own pocket.

Reserve Fund: You probably will have a monthly payment to a reserve fund which is saved for major repairs. Find out how much the monthly payment is and what the major repairs are likely to be. If this is an apartment project turned into a condominium, the property may be years old and all sorts of things could be ready to fall apart. You could have major expenses for repairs the next few years which would negate the financial advantage that was your reason for buying.

Who Owns Joint Facilities? Find out if the goodies connected with the condominium such as swimming pools, tennis courts, and saunas are going to be yours or the developer's. It could make a difference in the future.

When Do You Become Owner? If you're going to be part owner of the joint facilities, find out exactly when your ownership goes into effect. Developers sometimes hold onto the project until it's completely full. This means you have no voice in the way things are managed.

Investigate Project: In fact be very careful about buying into a partially completed condominium project. There have been cases where partially filled condominiums went bankrupt. To avoid this, investigate the financing behind the project if the one you're interested in is only partly sold. Ask who owns it, then look up the firm's reputation. You can check it by talking with the business editors of newspapers, officials of the local Home Builders Association, chamber of commerce officials, and your banker.

Management: Find out too who's going to manage the building. Good management can make all the difference in a condominium. Are you going to have to wait three days to get the elevator fixed every time it breaks down? If the heating goes off in your living room, how long till it comes back on? Are the public facilities going to be kept neat and tidy? Ask about other buildings this management has handled and take the time to check them out. It's too late to check once you're already in the building.

Guards, Pets and Children: Are there any security arrangements? What about pets? Can you bring your dog into the condominium or are pets and children frowned upon? Make sure you know all these answers before actually buying.

WHAT TO LOOK FOR IN A HOUSE

Make sure you know how old and in what state of repair are the following structural features:

* roof
* plumbing
* foundations and basements
* insulation, heating, and air-conditioning units
* yard and fences

These are the big five which can cost you a lot of money if they're not right. If you're planning to get a government loan, some of these things will be checked by officials. Ask your realtor which ones will be examined by lending officials. Check the others yourself.

If you buy an older home, you may get into really extensive repairs, new roofs, cracked slabs, leaking cellars. These are the kinds of repairs which run into thousands of dollars. A house, like a car, or for that matter a person, becomes more expensive to maintain as it ages. Maintenance and repair for a new house may run next to nothing, not counting the yard. For a 10-year-old house, it may run $300 to $400 a year.

Two General Rules: First, don't buy the biggest house on the block. It will be harder to resell than the smallest house on the block. Second, the front of a subdivision usually is less desirable than the middle and back.

Watch for Bargains: Keep an eye out for bargains, although they don't come along very often. You may be lucky enough to find a house where the owner has a low equity which he is willing to sell. That means you can pay for the equity and assume his loan, which saves several hundred dollars in closing costs and lets you make a lower down payment than you could get with a new loan. Also the existing loan may have a lower interest rate than you could get currently. This kind of bargain doesn't come on the market very often and when it does, it doesn't last long because everybody's looking for the same sort of deal.

Second Mortgage: Another way to avoid the standard down payment is to find an owner who will take a second mortgage or second lien. This is legal in most states. It works this way. Suppose the owner had $12,000 equity in his house and was making payments of $225 a month. You'd like the monthly payments of only $225 but you don't have $12,000 you need to pay him to assume his loan. He may be willing to take $6,000 and carry a personal loan with you for the remaining $6,000. Or you may be able to make the loan at a bank. That pushes your monthly payments up, since you're repaying the mortgage loan plus the second mortgage, but only for the length of time it takes to pay the $6,000.

Repossession: The third real bargain in home buying is a repossession, a home which a mortgage company has repossessed because the buyers didn't make their payments. These sell for very low amounts, far under market value.

TOWNHOUSE

Check

- Quality of structure
- Maintenance fee and what it covers
- Management—Do they have a good reputation for taking care of outside maintenance?
- Any restrictions such as children and pets

Go to a Realtor

You'll save time and energy if you turn over the initial looking to a realtor. Tell him what you want, where you want it, and what you can afford.

Be very firm about how much you can afford. Realtors, like other salesmen, may want to show you homes $10,000 more than your top figure on the theory that you can scare up the money if you try hard enough. Besides, the higher the sale price, the higher their commission. Don't look at more expensive homes. It's like shopping for clothes. If you look at the originals first, the dresses on the racks look tacky. Stay within your price range while you're looking.

Lending Agencies

Your realtor can suggest lending agencies to you. These include:

* banks
* mortgage companies
* savings and loans
* insurance companies

Lending officials want to know your income and any outstanding debts you may have. Agencies use various rules of thumb to determine if you can afford a home. One formula is one week's salary minus fixed debt should at least equal one month's mortgage payment.

annual income	$18,000
Subtract	
fixed debt (car payment)	1,200
	$16,800
Divide the remainder by	
52 weeks	$323

By this formula you can afford to buy a home where the mortgage payment is $323 per month. That includes loan interest, taxes, insurance, and mortgage principal.

Check with at least three lending organizations to see what kind of loan arrangement you can make. Not all lending agencies charge the same amount for loans.

If you're very short of money, you won't have much shopping room. You'll have to take whatever loan you can get, whether it's the best deal or not. If you're turned down, don't give up. Go to another lending agency. I know people who have gone to three and four lending agencies before they found one who would do business with them. But eventually they got their loans. Again your realtor may be able to help because she's probably been through this with other people.

Aids in Making Loans: As I said in the loan section, if your income is considered inadequate for a loan, you may be able still to make the loan by offering collateral (real estate, stocks, bonds) or you may be able to find someone to co-sign the note with you.

Get a Long-Term Loan: Remember to aim at the longest term loan you can get. Twenty-year loans are the norm but thirty-year loans are available and there's talk of forty-year loans. The longer you have to pay off the loan, the lower your monthly payments, the less equity you build. The less equity you build, the easier it is to resell. An exception is if you intend to keep the home the rest of your life and want to get it paid for as soon as possible. Then you may prefer a shorter term loan.

Attorney Should Read Contract: It is a very good idea to have your attorney read the loan contract before you sign it. Your realtor may arrange this. If you buy directly from an owner, make sure you have your attorney check the contract in case there's something wrong with it or with the title that you need to know before signing.

HOMEOWNERS INSURANCE

Along with your loan, you'll get homeowners insurance. Lending agencies have arrangements with different insurance companies to sell a standard homeowners policy.

You'll probably do better if you go to an insurance agency. William Burkhalter, a friend and one of my insurance advisers, points out that insurance people are in the business of selling insurance, not making loans. They may be able to give you a better policy or save you money in a way the lending agency would not.

Different policies cover different things but basically your homeowners policy should cover 80 percent of the value of the dwelling. If it burned down the insurance should be sufficient to pay 80 percent of the cost of rebuilding. Mortgage people may require insurance for as much as 90 percent of the value of the dwelling.

Damage to or Theft of Personal Possessions up to a certain percentage is covered by homeowners insurance. In case of fire insurance would pay a portion of the estimated value of your furniture, clothes, etc. The percentage ranges between 35 and 50 and varies with states.

Premise Medical, another standard provision, is similar but covers your being at fault. Suppose a deliveryman slipped on your sidewalk, fell, and twisted his back. He might sue for medical bills. Premise liability usually covers up to $25,000.

If you want more liability, you pay more, and it might not be a bad idea. It's quite inexpensive. Suits have mounted in number and amount the past few years. People frequently sue not only for their medical bills but for time lost from work. Suppose the deliveryman with the twisted back claims he can no longer drive a truck. His live-lihood is gone. He could be out of work for years. He could sue for thousands of dollars and might collect.

Question your insurance agent about the liability necessary in your area.

Off-Premise Damage. Some policies also cover household goods when they're temporarily off premise. If you send a couch to be recovered, the truck has an accident and the new upholstery is ripped, the insurance company will pay part of the cost of mending or replacing.

Climatic Disasters. Another important provision in homeowners insurance should be climatic disasters common to your area. Most policies cover wind and water damage. But if you live on a coast, you'll want coverage for hurricanes. In California, for earthquakes. In the south and middlewest, for tornadoes.

Condominium Insurance is much the same as that for house and townhouse except it covers only personal possessions and inside walls. It may be a group policy covering all units or you may have to buy individual insurance.

Mortgage Cancellation. When you buy homeowners insurance, the agent may suggest you also buy a policy that pays the mortgage in full if the owner dies. This is called mortgage cancellation insurance. Actually it's life insurance, term or decreasing term, and can be a rider attached to your regular life insurance. The cost depends on the age of the insured.

If you're single and have no heirs to whom you want to leave a home, obviously you couldn't care less whether or not the mortgage is paid in full if you die, so skip it.

However if you have dependents, you may want to buy this insurance to leave your heirs the security of a home that's paid for. By the time you're in your forties or fifties, you definitely need this insurance if you have a large mortgage on your home. If the mortgage is almost paid, insurance is not too important. Take care of your health and put the money into investments instead.

CAPITAL GAINS TAX

Eventually you may decide to sell your home. You've had a tax advantage all the years you owned it but when you sell, you must think about capital gains tax. This is a tax on any profit you make on a sale.

Let's say you live in a home for which you paid $30,000 10 years ago and decide to sell. You've kept the home in good condition but property values haven't gone up so you can probably expect to sell it for about what you paid for it. The buyers refinance the home. This means they get a new loan of $24,000 or so. You pay the mortgage company what you still owe them, which leaves you with about $8,000.

This $8,000 will be taxed as capital gains if you don't buy another home within 18 months. Or if you're building a home, the government allows 24 months before they tax the $8,000. If you buy or build a more expensive home within that time period, you won't pay capital gains. If you buy or build a less expensive home, you'll be taxed on the difference.

Suppose you sold your home for $60,000 and bought a $40,000 townhouse. You have to pay tax on the difference, $20,000. Capital gains taxes only half your profit so that means you're taxed on $10,000. Then you have to pay 15 percent on the other half of the profit. But there's an exemption for $10,000 or half your income tax, whichever is greater. It becomes very complicated, as you can see. The point to remember is if you're making a good-sized profit, you can save a lot of money if you receive your payment over a period of years instead of in a lump sum. If the profit is spread out in installments, you pay less tax.

WHEN SHOULD YOU SELL?

You may want to sell and buy another home for any number of reasons.

- You could have a baby and need a larger home
- The children could grow up, leave, and you need a smaller one
- Your work might necessitate your moving to another city
- Your home may need so much repair that it would be cheaper to buy another than repair this one
- The neighborhood might be deteriorating
- You may just be tired of your home and want a change
- You may want to sell if you're widowed or divorced, although don't think you must get rid of your home just because you become single after being married. You may prefer to stay. You need time to get your financial affairs sorted to see if keeping the home is a good financial move.

Some women cling to their homes like snails to a shell. Others want to be free of as much responsibility as possible. If you have children, consider whether the home will provide a measure of security for them in a period of emotional upheaval. Make certain how you feel before making any move, if you can possibly delay it.

Sometimes a woman may prefer to leave a home but the thought of preparing it for sale is so overwhelming that she can't face it. Don't let inertia keep you in a home you don't want. You can cope if you really try.

Call a good realtor whose advice you can trust, show her around and through the house and ask what needs to be done to make it marketable.

The realtor may suggest you do some repainting and repapering, even recarpeting. She may also suggest you put some of your furniture in storage so things won't be so crowded. Some houses show to best advantage when they're furnished, others don't. Follow her advice—within reason. Don't of course spend too much on redoing. You want to make some kind of profit on the sale.

It's more fun to have painting and papering done when you're going to enjoy them, but look at it as a business transaction. Think of the home objectively, not as the place you've put so much of yourself into but as a piece of real estate to be displayed to its best advantage. Make a schedule for yourself to get things done and start as soon as possible. You'll find your satisfaction at doing the job more than compensates for lack of interest in the home itself.

WHAT ABOUT A CAR?

Another important consideration is transportation. If you live in a city where public transport is good so a car is unnecessary, you'll save both money and bother. But if you live outside highly urbanized areas, a car is only slightly less important than a home.

What to Buy

Factors you need to consider when buying a car include:

- cost
- gas consumption
- resale value
- personal needs and preferences
- depreciation
- maintenance and repairs
- safety features

Original cost. An automobile is the second most expensive item most people buy. At this writing, the cost of a new car ranged from $3,150 up. The least expensive cars now available are sub-compacts and small foreign autos. Compacts are the next least expensive; then large cars, sports models, limousines, rare old models, custom-made autos, and high-priced foreign cars.

Depreciation. After the original purchase price, the next highest cost of a new car is depreciation. It runs about 30 percent of the original cost the first year, about 18 percent the second. Third-year depreciation begins to level off at around 13 percent and fourth-year about 9 percent. So if you pay $4,000 for a car, depreciation the first year is about $1,200, about $500 the second year.

Gasoline consumption is another major consideration when choosing a car, not only because of the high cost of fuel but because of the need to conserve it. Laws may be passed to limit the amount of gas a car can consume, or to charge extra for big gas users, but at this writing, you must depend upon yourself to check gas use of any car you're considering buying.

Maintenance and repair can be expensive, time consuming, and inconvenient. You can check a particular model's record of repair in *Consumer Reports'* April and December issues, available both at the library and on newsstands. The reports don't mean an individual car will behave like the average, but they're one of the few guides we have.

Resale value is another cost consideration when you buy. The more popular a car, the easier it will be to resell. You may get a bargain on an odd model, but you'll also receive less when you resell or trade it in.

Safety features are listed in pamphlets and sales persons have them available.

Specific needs and personal preferences. You'll also want to take these into account when buying. If you travel a great deal, you probably want a big car with good springs that makes a long drive as comfortable as possible. If you're an artist and haul paintings hither and yon, or the mother of many, you may need a station wagon. If you live on a farm, a pickup truck. If you do most of your driving back and forth to work, classes, shopping, and so on, you can get along with a medium-sized car which uses little gasoline, moves neatly through traffic, and is easy to park.

The kind of car you prefer expresses your opinion of yourself as plainly as do the clothes you buy. If you have a stately dignified image of yourself, you'll prefer a stately, dignified car. If you're an energetic, on-the-go person, you're more likely to want a zippier car. If you're a student and very young, you probably prefer small cars, preferably foreign. Since a car is expensive, preferences may be one thing and ability to purchase another. Even if your self-image is best expressed by a custom-designed Rolls-Royce, you may find it more practicable to settle for a plain, American-made auto.

Before Buying a Car

1) Read any material available on cost and performance of new cars. You can find information at the public library and on news-stands.

2) Decide how much you can spend and how long you plan to keep the car.

To Save Money When Buying

1) Wait until new models arrive toward the end of the year and buy the current model. This makes your car a year old while it's brand new; you can save several hundred dollars, and it still drives like a new car.

2) Since depreciation is highest when a car is new, plan to keep it several years. If you do a great deal of traveling, you need a car every two or three years. If not, you can usually make do five or six years or even longer.

3) Know how much a car should cost before you start looking. You can check in *Consumer Reports* or compare prices at different dealers.

4) Sometimes you can go to a small town and find better prices than in the city. If you have shopping time, this might be worth trying.

At the Dealer's

Be sure and ask the total price of the car. Otherwise you may be quoted the cost of the car alone not counting taxes, delivery prices, and final car prep such as undercoating.

Drive the car both in traffic and at a higher speed. Listen for an unevenness or odd sounds in the motor.

Check to make sure the following work: horn, windshield wipers, all gauges on dashboard, cigarette lighter, any other devices, heater and air-conditioner, if they're included.

Is anything broken or rickety inside the car, such as handles or door locks? Any dents or scratches outside? Look at the chrome as well as the body. Any outstanding rattles?

Have all repairs done before you accept delivery of the car even though the dealer promises to complete repairs in the future in one day at your convenience.

Study the warranty to see what it covers and how long it lasts.

Read your service manual and follow instructions. Your car will function much better if you take regular care of it.

Used Cars

Buying a used car is risky unless you know about motors or know someone who will examine a car for you. Even at best, a used car is almost sure to develop major motor problems before a new one, so if you can possibly afford it, buy a new one.

If you must buy a used car, the market price of any car is listed in the *Official Used Car Guide* published by the National Automobile Dealers Association or *The Kelly Auto Market Report* (Blue Book). These are available at dealers and at most banks.

Neither would I recommend foreign cars. They're fun but they have things go wrong just like the homemade cars and there are fewer mechanics who can repair them. You also may wait a long time for parts.

Taxes and Your Auto

When you figure your income tax, be sure to deduct any taxes you paid for your car. If you borrow money to buy the car, you can also deduct interest on the loan.

If your car is used in connection with your work, aside from normal going and coming, you can take further deductions. Talk with your accountant to determine current deductions.

Resale

Each car has an individual health span having to do with its upkeep, environment, heritage, and quality of parts. Some cars are still purring along reliably at 100,000 miles. Others are in and out of the shop all their lives. The best time to trade is just before you start having major repairs, the kind that cost $250, $300, and up. If you don't trade the car in before you have the big repairs, you may as well drive it another year to absorb the repair cost. Unless, that is, you suspect some other catastrophic repair is imminent.

Each time you have a check-up, ask your mechanic to examine everything and warn you if he suspects a problem with something potentially expensive, like the transmission. If your time is valuable, you can lose more money waiting to get your car repaired than you lose trading it in early and taking the depreciation loss.

Trade-In?

You can probably make a profit if you sell your car yourself instead of trading it in on a new car. However it takes time, effort, and some expense. You have to advertise it, be on hand to show it, and dicker with potential buyers. Even then, you probably will make only around $100 more than if you traded it in.

Before reselling or trading in, check to see what the market value is. You can expect to get market value if your car is in top condition for its age.

If you trade the car in on a new one, you should deduct its market value from the cost of the new one and pay the difference. However, dealers like to bargain with trade-ins. Some say they will pay more than your car is worth as a trade-in. Others offer less than it's worth but drop the price of the new car. Regardless of what the dealer says, the end figures should be the same, market value of old car deducted from cost of new one.

You probably will get a better deal if you stay with the same car brand. If you've got a big car, you probably will do better financially if you buy another big one. It's hard to trade down. A smaller car trades about as well on the same size or larger.

CAR INSURANCE

Even if your state doesn't require auto insurance, buy it. You can't afford to drive without insurance. An accident where either you or another person was seriously injured could wipe you out financially.

William E. Burkhalter of Southwest General Insurance Agency, Houston, has spoken at many of my seminars about insurance. He and Perry Smith, senior marketing representative of the Insurance Company of North America, advised me on insurance needed for adequate protection. There is variation among states as to amounts and requirements.

Liability insurance covers bodily injury to other persons and damage to their property in an accident which is your fault. If you have an accident and it's the other driver's fault, his liability insurance should cover your damages or injuries. People sue for astronomical amounts for bodily injuries. Settlements of $100,000 are not unusual and some have run as high as $300,000. Talk with your agent about how much to buy.

The coverage you need for property damage usually is much less because even if you had an accident and a brand-new car was destroyed, you'd still need less than $20,000 to pay for it.

You could buy a policy that would pay up to $100,000 for bodily injuries and up to $300,000 per accident. That is, if a person was injured and could never work again, he might sue for half a million. The insurance would pay $300,000 of that. Or if two persons were injured and each sued for $100,000, the insurance would pay both of them.

Collision insurance pays for damage to your own car if the accident wasn't caused by somebody else or if the other driver had no insurance. This is a deductible policy and $200 deductible is about average. You can buy more coverage with $100 deductible but it costs more. A $300 deductible costs less. If you have a new car and want to make sure you can afford to keep it undented, you may want a lower deductible. But if your car is aging, you're well enough protected with $250 or even $300 deductible.

Comprehensive insurance covers theft or damage to your vehicle other than an accident. Comprehensive pays for repair if high winds blow a tree over onto your car, or if your hubcaps are stolen. This too is a deductible and ranges from $50 to $250.

Two other policies are worth consideration. One is *Personal Injury Protection*. This is for you in case you're hurt in an accident. It usually runs about $2,500 and pays your medical bills and loss of income to that amount, or however much your policy is worth. It pays immediately, which most policies don't.

Uninsured motorist coverage protects you if you're injured by someone who has no insurance. It pays $10,000 to $20,000 and costs only about $6 or $7 a year.

Car insurance rates are the same for women and men, married and single. Rates go up if a person under twenty-five or over sixty-five habitually drives the car.

The amount of insurance you need depends upon how much and where you drive. If you live in a small town where there are few accidents, you can get along with minimum coverage. If you live in a metropolitan area where traffic is fast and crowded, you need more. Discuss your needs with your insurance agent. He can help you decide how much to buy.

Anyone who drives a car with permission of the owner is covered by the owner's insurance on most policies.

SERVICE AND REPAIR

While your car is under warranty, take it back to the dealer for any repairs covered by the warranty.

Try to find a service station near you which you like, and go to it regularly. Station attendants can help you keep an eye on the car's condition.

When the warranty ends, you may or may not want to return to the dealer for servicing and repair. An advantage to going to the dealer is that mechanics should be familiar with your brand of car and know exactly how to repair it. A disadvantage is that dealers usually charge higher fees than smaller mechanic shops. They also are so large that you're unlikely ever to know the people or they you. It's an advantage to know your mechanic and be able to trust him in his diagnosis of your car's ailments. Even if you do have a good relationship with a mechanic, if he tells you your car needs some major repair costing $100 or more, check it with another mechanic before having the work done.

Always ask the price of any work before having it done, even minor things like oil changes and wheel balancing. Otherwise you may be charged exorbitantly and if the work is already done, it's too late to say it's too much.

If a garage is having a special on something like oil changes, tell the mechanic that's what you came in for. Otherwise you may get a super duper job that doesn't qualify for the special.

Things You Should Do for Your Car

You may spend three or four weeks shopping before you buy a car but you'll spend years maintaining it so it may help to know a few of the basics of car maintenance.

It's a good idea to take a course in rudimentary auto mechanics. They're offered at places like the "Y." If you're still in school, take it one semester as an elective. Knowing just the simple things about your car can save time, money, and inconvenience in the future. Nothing is more irritating than spending all afternoon sitting around a garage waiting for your car to be repaired.

A course showing you the little things every driver should know about her car can save what during a lifetime probably amounts to about a month of dire boredom and frustration. You'll learn all sorts of helpful hints.

When you're driving along a nice smooth road, every once in

a while take your hands off the steering wheel. Does the car immediately head for a curb or angle madly toward an oncoming car? If so your wheels are probably out of alignment and will wear the tires out rapidly if you don't get them straightened.

Does the battery have water? You can't tell for sure unless you look in each of the little holes. One can be empty while the others have water. If it is, it's called a dry cell and your car will refuse to start someday when you have someplace very important to go and a minimum amount of time to get there.

Are your car's tires thick and round or thin and flabby? A flabby tire can turn into a floppy tire and cause your car to thud sickeningly as you tool along. If you continue to drive on it, the tire will be cut into pieces and you'll have to buy a new one. A thin tire may wear a hole in itself and you'll have a blowout when you're driving.

Other things to watch for on tires are thinning places on just one part of one tire. That means all four tires aren't going around the same way. One of them is out of balance. Most service stations can balance wheels.

Always keep air in your spare tire. If you have a flat on a lonely road and your spare is flat too, you're in a sad situation.

If you're driving along and water appears on your windshield when it's not raining, the water hose has probably burst. Or if you hear a funny whiny sound, the hose that's connected to the fuel pump may have broken. You should examine your hoses every six months or so. If they don't look firm and elastic, stop by a garage and ask a mechanic to look at them. When they start serious aging, it's best to replace them instead of waiting for a rupture.

The oil should be changed every 10,000 miles because it gets dirty and deposits little particles of slush in the motor. When the station changes the oil, they put a stickon paper on the door facing on the driver's side of the car with date and current mileage written on. If a mechanic tells you the oil is dirty, check your record and see if 10,000 miles or close to it have rolled over on the odometer. If so, have an oil change. If not, check with another mechanic.

Once in a while you should check your transmission fluid if you have automatic transmission.

Put anti-freeze in the radiator before cold weather. Everything should be all right then both that winter and the next. However, if your radiator starts acting up and boils over, you may lose the anti-freeze and have to put in more. Attendants at stations have gauges with which they can measure the amount of anti-freeze in the radiator. You can buy anti-freeze at supermarkets and pour it into the radiator yourself, thereby saving several dollars. However, if you're busy and think you may put it off, have it put in at a station and pay the price. It's better than letting your car freeze.

If your temperature gauge goes up to "H" for "Hot," you've got a problem. It can be a variety of things so get to a mechanic immediately. It's probably the radiator but it could be other things. You can nurse a car along for months and it will run a fever only upon occasion, but one day it will give a low gasp and the motor will quit.

Any time a car develops whines, ticks, or thumps, it needs to go to the mechanic. The ailment may go away if you wait but it probably won't. It'll probably get worse and may affect something else.

Think of your car as your friend. Try to understand the reasons for its eccentricities. Remember that when a car behaves worst, it needs attention most.

Now let's review.

QUIZ

1. I'm only twenty-five. I think it's much too early for me to worry about health and disability insurance.

You need health and disability insurance unless someone else would pay in case you were injured or ill.

2. I don't know how much emergency funds I need. What do most people have?

I recommend emergency funds sufficient to pay all your expenses for three to six months, depending upon your age and personal need for security.

3. You keep talking about long-range goals and they seem like a good idea but I have no idea what I want to do at sixty-five. That's thirty years from now.

Do you want to live where you do now? Do you want to do the same things that you are doing now? Or do you want to expand your life and be doing something else? Are you an indoor or outdoor person? Do you want to spend your life on city activities or fishing and gardening or what? Your long-range goals must be based upon your personal desires. Once you decide what you want to be doing in the future, figure how much it will cost—that gives you a long-range financial goal.

4. I'm considering buying a condominium apartment in a project which is about half full. How can I be sure this is a good place to buy?

Check the financing and people behind the project. Talk with your banker and attorney. If you decide to proceed, make sure your contract provides that you recover your money should the project fail.

5. If it's cheaper to buy than to rent, why doesn't everyone buy?

Some people never can afford the down payment. Some don't want the responsibilities of ownership. Some move so much that it would be impractical for them to buy.

6. Are the tax advantages as good on a townhouse and condominium as on a house?

Yes.

7. I've known people who bought homes and then couldn't keep up the payments. Their mortgage payments are no more than the apartment rent they were paying previously. How does this happen?

They didn't consider the hidden costs in home buying. These can amount to a great deal, especially the first year.

8. My realtor said I would be able to get a loan to buy a townhouse, but I've been turned down by two banks. What can I do?

Go to a third bank. Or to a savings and loan, mortgage company, or insurance company.

9. I know I could keep up payments on a home because I'm very careful with my money but lenders don't think my income is adequate. Where can I get a loan?

Offer collateral if you have it. Or get someone to co-sign the note with you.

10. I've found a home with a mortgage interest rate of 6½ percent. If I keep the lower cost mortgage, I'll have to pay a second lien. Is this a good idea?

If a second lien is legal in your state, and if you can afford to make both mortgage payments, it would save money in the long run to take the better loan.

11. The mortgage company where I'm financing my home offers an insurance policy. Should I buy it?

You'll probably do better to go to an insurance company that specializes in homeowners insurance.

12.   Is liability insurance on a home really necessary?

Yes. If someone should be hurt on the premises, you could be sued. You need to be protected by liability insurance.

13.   If I sell my home and buy a more expensive one within 18 months, do I have to pay capital gains tax?

No.

14.   My car is listed in the *Blue Book* as being worth $900 but I can't find a dealer who will value it at more than $750.

Perhaps your car is in poor condition. If no dealer will pay the list price, take the highest offer you can get.

15.   My car is only four years old but two mechanics have told me I'm probably going to have major repairs within the next 10,000 miles. Should I trade it in now or risk paying the repairs?

That depends on how valuable your time is and how much the repairs will cost. Figure how much time you're likely to lose taking the car back and forth to mechanics. Count in hauling charges if your insurance doesn't cover that. Try to estimate cost of repairs. Compare the figures to see which is greater. Another consideration is whether or not you can afford to buy a new car at this time.

16.   What are the three kinds of insurance every driver needs?

Liability, collision, comprehensive. They may have slightly different names in different states.

17.   I had to buy new tires and the sales person said they'd cost $44 each but they wound up being almost $50 each.

When you buy tires, as when you buy a car, ask the total price. Tires are taxed, which pushes up the price several dollars.

18.   My brother changes his own oil. Is there any reason I can't?

None at all. You have to crawl under the car and you need a container for the old motor oil to run into. You can save several dollars by doing your own oil changes. Be sure and keep records of the dates.

Money for Your Heirs

Conserving an Estate with a Will

The purpose of a will is to make sure that your estate goes to the heirs of your choice, and there's some of the estate left for heirs.

A will not only *distributes* your estate but if written correctly *conserves* it. If it is written incorrectly, an unnecessarily large portion of your holdings can be eaten up by taxes.

Even though you're young, you should understand wills because you may be an heir. You may be able to give your parents or other relatives tips that will conserve their estates. Remember, if the estate doesn't go to heirs, it goes to the IRS, state government, or, if you get into legal battles, attorneys. So you as an heir will deprive no one by helping your older relatives write a will.

The average man spends more than 11,000 days of his life working to make money. But he thinks it's a waste of time to take off one day to make a will so that his family will be provided for when he dies. The average woman spends an untold number of days of her life working but fewer women than men have wills.

Almost one third of the business and professional men in the nation have no will. Twice that many wives have no will, although when a widow dies, her estate probably will be diminished much more than it was when her husband died.

A study in the San Francisco area showed that seven out of every eight adults died without a valid will. Less than half of those persons with estates over $60,000 had a will.

Parents will give minor children every advantage they're able to give but leave their entire future to chance by not making a will. They should make both financial provisions and name a guardian to look after the youngsters' welfare.

Some people think wills are necessary only for the rich. If you think you don't own enough to bother making a will, add up your assets. They may total more than you realized. Even if your estate is relatively insignificant, you want it to go to those persons you care for or perhaps a church or charitable institution. I have yet to meet anyone who wanted her estate to go to the tax collector, but that's what is likely to happen if you don't prepare.

Government inherits enormous amounts of money each year because people neglect to set their affairs in order with a proper will. If you want your family to benefit from your estate, make a valid will.

WHAT TO CONSIDER WHEN MAKING A WILL

The first consideration for survivors is the funeral and burial of the deceased. You can figure immediate costs of about $3,000 for these if you haven't already bought a burial plot. If the decedent is entitled to burial benefits from Social Security or if a veteran, perhaps from the Veterans Administration, some of these costs can be diminished.

Debts against the estate become due when the property holder dies.

If the estate is subject to federal tax, that must be paid. The IRS allows nine months for payments. If heirs can't get tax money together in that time, the government will grant an extension. Interest is charged on the unpaid sum in accordance with a formula which is predicated on the prime rate at any given time.

The state also may tax the estate. Taxes go by different names in different states—estate tax, inheritance tax, or death tax. The only state without one is Nevada.

Liquid Funds

It is most important that your estate include enough liquid funds to pay these immediate debts. Remember that bank accounts may be frozen at the time of death. Safe deposit boxes are sealed.

Without liquid funds, heirs may have to pay debts themselves, if they are able. If they aren't, they may have to sell real estate, stocks, bonds, something of value. Forced sales are rarely profitable. That's how estates are lost.

How to Provide Liquid Funds

A good way to make sure you have cash on hand in your estate is with life insurance. If a life policy is large enough to cover funeral and burial costs, debts and taxes, your survivors won't have to sell something valuable.

Another protection is to take out term insurance on any major loan so the debt will be paid in case of death.

An estate consisting entirely of real estate—unless it's a working farm or ranch—presents a major cash problem. Obligations simply cannot be met except by mortgaging the property or selling it in a hurry, consequently usually at a sacrifice.

In order to have cash on hand to satisfy debts and taxes, your lawyer may suggest you sell some property yourself instead of waiting until heirs are forced to sell.

Line of Inheritance

After debts and taxes are paid, the remainder of the estate goes to heirs. If you die intestate, without a will, the state determines who inherits.

The usual line of inheritance goes spouse, children, siblings, parents, nieces and nephews, cousins, anybody as long as they're a living, breathing relative. But that's "usual"; you can't count on it. Generally a wife inherits a husband's estate and vice versa if there are no children.

If there are children, the wife usually inherits a portion and the children inherit a portion. Most community property states decree that if there is more than one minor child, a wife inherits one-third of the estate and the children two-thirds. This sounds fine on paper but in reality it can become a sticky wicket. I had a client who was caught in this trap. She couldn't even sell her deceased husband's car although the children were too young to drive and she didn't need two cars. She had to appear before a judge and prove that selling the second car would not deplete the children's estate.

Imagine the complications involved when there is more than one marriage and children from each union. If a will isn't written comprehensively, some of the children, or maybe the widow, depending upon the state, are disinherited. Suppose a couple has three children. They divorce. Ten years later the man remarries and the new wife produces two offspring. He's got youngsters in their twenties and preschool children. If he dies without a will, who's going to inherit? Probably the current wife and her children. The first children may be left out entirely.

One young woman who came for counseling told me her husband had just learned from his attorney that in case both he and she died in a common disaster, since they were childless, his brothers would inherit their property. His parents would receive nothing although they were in need. The couple quickly had a will drawn to protect the older people.

Disinherited

A man or woman living together but not formally married have no legal claims on property if one of them dies. However I've heard of one court case where the judge awarded the estate to the survivor.

Children whose parents aren't married don't inherit if they're not written into the will. They may sue for a portion of the estate but that's no guarantee that they will be awarded it.

Do It Now

Make your will now while you're incontestably alert and brimming with vigor. That's probably one of the obstacles to making a will. We feel so good we think there's no point in it. Or we feel so badly, we feel too melancholy to do it. It's the old story of the broken window—can't fix it in the rain and don't need it in the sunshine.

Another reason you shouldn't wait is that if your will is made within three years of your death, some of your bequests might be questioned and taxed. Tax laws state that if you give away holdings within three years of your death, you are giving them away "in contemplation of death"—that's the legal phrase—in order to avoid maximum taxation. So do the will immediately.

It is important to work closely with a lawyer who's up on the law and can advise you knowledgeably how best to conserve your estate. I've learned however that people put off doing this. So I suggest you first . . .

Make a Handwritten Will

It will help you organize your thinking, learn the current value of your holdings, and save several hours of your attorney's time. Since attorneys usually charge by the hour this saves you money.

List the following:

- Your name and any variations
- Permanent residence and any secondary addresses
- Date and place of birth
- Wife's or husband's name and same information as 1, 2, and 3
- Have you been previously married? Full information concerning marriage termination
- Names and addresses of immediate family (sons, daughters, parents)
- Have you ever created a trust? Are you the beneficiary under a trust or will?
- Has anyone ever given you the authority to name the beneficiaries under a trust or will?
- Name of employer
- Any pension, profit sharing, or other benefits
- Complete information on all insurance policies: company, numbers, beneficiaries (primary and secondary); include any group policies
- Complete list of assets: estimate current market value and how registered or titled
- List any outstanding debts including mortgages
- Are you covered by Blue Cross-Blue Shield, Medicare, or some other medical insurance?
- Location of your last three years' income tax returns, stocks, bonds, deeds, savings account passbooks, etc.
- Location of safe deposit box and key
- Names and addresses of proposed executor, guardian, and trustee, if any
- Most importantly, your plans for your beneficiaries

Remember this is only an interim document. It's just going to tide you over until you can make an appointment with your attorney. Handwritten wills aren't legal in a few states, but they're recognized in many and they're better than nothing.

A woman about forty years of age attended one of my seminars. She said that she and her husband had no wills and her husband wouldn't even consider making one. He was forty-one and felt that he was too young to be bothered. He'd make a will when he was older.

I strongly recommended that she try to get him to make a handwritten will, but he refused. Six months later he died after a heart attack. Their financial affairs were in a tangle and the amount of money she had to spend getting them straightened out was out of all proportion to the amount she stood to inherit. Even a handwritten will would have saved her several thousand dollars.

Children

List your children by name in your will. Don't say simply that you want your children to share equally in your estate. List each one by full name.

If you have minor children, name a guardian in your will. It never ceases to amaze me that people will do everything in their power for children except make provisions for a home for them in case both parents die. Couples will fly off to Acapulco leaving the kids at home with a sitter. If the plane crashes, the children are left without a home.

Decide whom you want as a guardian. Discuss the matter with that person to make sure she or he is agreeable. Acting as guardian for children is a chore because the court requires close record keeping to determine how money is being spent and whether it's to the children's advantage or not. Every little point has to be taken up with a judge, and most people don't want to go to all that trouble.

If you make no provision for children in a will, the court decides who will care for them. Even if relatives decide among themselves, the court must approve.

Anytime minors are included in your will, whether your own children, grandchildren, or whatever, it's a good idea to leave the inheritance in trust. I'll go into this in detail later.

Be sure to include the statement that this will revokes any previous wills or any in existence at this time and that this is the only will as of the date of this instrument.

The second worst thing to having no will probably is having too many. The plethora of wills that turned up following the death of Howard Hughes is an outstanding example.

Even two can be too many. A young client told me that she was made executor of her uncle's will. Apparently the uncle was the kind of person everybody liked and he liked everybody. He liked everybody so much that when some friends suggested he make a will leaving them his business, he agreed, although he had already made a will leaving his estate to his family. When he died, nobody was sure which of the two wills was valid.

My client paid funeral and burial costs herself. It was either that or have the state bury her uncle because his money was tied up in the dispute. She hired an attorney who couldn't seem to get anything done. Then she hired another attorney and was hoping finally to get the matter settled. It had drifted on at this point for 18 months.

"The trouble with Uncle Clarence," she kept saying, "was that he just loved everybody."

So watch too much loving. Make sure your latest will revokes any previous ones.

Common Disaster Clause

If you're married, be sure to include in your will what is called a "common disaster" clause. This means that if both spouses die in an accident, the wife or the husband should be named in the will as predeceasing. Which one should predecease depends upon which has the greater holdings.

Suppose both husband and wife are in a bus-train collision. Both are dead and nobody really knows when either died. Maybe the coroner found the husband's body at 12:01, identified him and signed the time on the death certificate. Ten minutes later he found the wife's body and listed her time of death as 12:10. Those are the times the probate court accepts so the law states that the estate passed from the husband to the wife for nine minutes. That's enough to have it taxed twice, and heirs would lose a lot of money.

Out-of-State Assets

If you have assets out of the state, bring them into the state where you live. This may avoid a lot of legal hassle.

Some states require ancillary administration on all tangible personal property, and some even for stocks, bonds, and bank accounts. Ancillary administration is the probate of a part of your estate in a state different from the one in which you live. Say you left a bank account in your home town and moved into another state. Your heirs might have to go through probate in the first state in order to obtain the bank account. This would require numerous letters, phone calls, probably a trip or two, and an extra attorney's fee before the thing was settled.

Real Estate

Real estate owned in another state presents a problem since you can hardly bring it into your home state. You can handle it in different ways.

- Make it an outright gift to your heirs
- Retain a life interest in the property, including the right to sell
- Place it in joint tenancy
- Place it in a revocable living trust

- Incorporate the property, if it is sizeable. This in effect converts it from real estate to stock, and in most states stock is not subject to ancillary administration

This is a detail that you will want to discuss with your lawyer; so, for the time being, simply list the real estate if you have any in your handwritten will.

Make the Will Self-Proving

By that I mean put a statement in the will saying, "You may prove that this is my signature by looking at the signature on my library card or ABC bank card. The library card is in my wallet; the signature card is with the bank." The reason for this is that you further identify yourself and prove that it is your intent to make a valid will.

Division of Property

Maybe one reason people put off making wills is that they don't know how to divide their property among heirs. The best way to think of your estate is in percentages. The entire estate is 100 percent. Think of it as a pie and apportion pieces of appropriate size to your heirs.

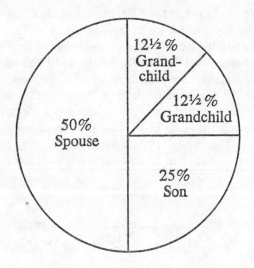

If you bequeath specific amounts to heirs, they may run into trouble. The value of holdings changes with inflation. Debts or taxes may be more than you anticipated. If you leave $50,000 after debts and taxes to your daughter, the estate may not contain $50,000 after those debts and taxes. In that case the state may decide what to do about the bequest. It may eliminate it entirely or it may work out a pro-rata distribution. Avoid such a possibility by leaving the estate in percentages.

Personal Belongings

Then there are personal belongings to think about. These are termed "chattel" and consist of everything in your estate except real estate. Every family has objects they value for sentimental reasons, if no other, and where there are several children, the distribution can get sticky. Sisters who have been devoted for 50 years may have a tiff over a teapot and not speak to each other for the next 50.

I know of a case where the sale of the deceased parent's home was held up for two years because the children—they're over fifty, every one of them—couldn't agree on dividing the personal belongings.

Attorneys finally settled the impasse by giving each heir colored tickets. One had blue, one red, one yellow, and so on. Each child went around the house and put tickets on items he wanted. Then the appraiser came through. He took everything with red tags and totaled them to get the dollar value. Then he totaled the blue, and the yellow. If he found that red totaled $51,372 and yellow totaled only $50,150, red had to give up something so the total could be even. It was either this or sell everything lock, stock, and barrel and divide the money equally. The children wouldn't hear of that because they wanted the objects themselves.

Another couple I know had a beautiful old round oak table, and each of their four children at one time or another mentioned he would like to have the table. Rather than have ill feelings in the future among the siblings, the couple sold the table to a stranger.

Letter of Intent

Many attorneys will recommend that distribution of your personal belongings, your wedding ring, the diamond pin Aunt Sarah used to wear, be an addendum to the will. Attach to the will a Letter of Intent and state in it who is to get what personal belongings. These aren't included in the property which is divided by percentages because usually these things have more sentimental than cash value. If personal belongings are included in the estate, you have to have appraisers value everything, and this can be expensive. Unless your things are worth a great deal the appraiser's charges may be more than the value of the item he is appraising.

Where personal belongings are concerned watch out for old friends of the deceased. I have a client who was settling up her aunt's estate and an elderly lady, seventy-five if she was a day, appeared and claimed that dear Catherine had promised her the twelve-place setting of Lenox. Dear Catherine had done no such thing. Another turned up claiming Catherine had promised a small chest to her. Since Catherine had been a very farsighted woman and listed all her personal belongings, my client was able to pacify the ladies with less valuable mementos.

SEAL THE ESTATE

It would have been easier for my client if the estate had been sealed. That would have allowed only the trustee or executor to enter the premises. This is a good idea because there are innumerable cases where relatives enter a house after a death and simply remove everything they want. They may not wait for reading of the will or anything else. They take while the taking is good. Even if you find the objects later, there's nothing you can do about them. You don't want to sue over Aunt Mary's sugar tongs, which is the sort of thing family members tend to appropriate. The items aren't worth a suit either financially or emotionally. Seal the estate, and avoid possible ill feeling.

WITNESSES

Get witnesses to your signature. This is not necessary in some cases but it never hurts. Choose people you know who are younger than you. People tend to have witnesses who are their contemporaries and as a consequence the witnesses are often dead before they can witness that your signature is a correct one. This is true of legal papers, including a will.

GO TO AN ATTORNEY

Once you get the handwritten will finished, make an appointment with your attorney and get a proper will made. Any number of things could cause a handwritten will to be invalid, such as:

1) inaccuracies of wording
2) duplications of meanings
3) your state could have quirky laws which you don't know about but your attorney does. The book *Wills of the U.S. Presidents* points out that President Calvin Coolidge was careful to write in his will,

"Not being unmindful of my son John, I leave all my estate both real and personal to my wife Grace Coolidge, in fee simple." The phrase about his son served the purpose of precluding a suit by John alleging his father had simply overlooked him.

How to Find a Reputable Attorney

If you don't have an attorney, call the American Bar Association and ask for recommendations. They'll probably give you at least three names. Call these and don't hesitate to ask how much they charge to draw up a will. Most don't mind quoting a fee but they'll have to know whether you have in mind a simple two-page will or a multi-pager.

The length will depend primarily on how complicated you make your division of property and how many heirs you include. Even a relatively small estate divided among ten persons requires a longish will. Also if you include particular stipulations, you add to the length. For instance I heard about the will of a very rich man who had a son and daughter. The son had been in some scrapes and showed signs of laziness and irresponsibility, so in the will the man left his daughter half the estate outright. But the son's half of the estate was set up so that he would be paid one dollar for every dollar he earned.

TAXES

In addition to drawing the will so that it is a valid legal document, your attorney can advise you about taxes to be expected. In 1976 Congress eliminated the estate tax, usually called an inheritance tax, and substituted the "transfer tax" which they identified as a charge for transferring belongings of the deceased to heirs.

The law also made most trusts subject to tax, eliminated exemptions and substituted for them "unified credits" which tax lawyers are still studying, and generally turned the inheritance scene fuzzy. One of the stated intentions was to make inheritance taxes more equitable.

The tax picture for the married shows that taking into account all possible deductions, an estate valued up to $425,000 may be exempt from federal taxes when a husband or wife dies. The survivor may take a $250,000 deduction or half the value of the estate, whichever is larger.

Home Deduction

The new law also allows deduction of half the price of a home if husband and wife own it jointly. It's considered a gift to the spouse. If half does exceed $100,000, the excess is taxed.

Jointly Owned Property

All jointly owned property except a house is taxed when a spouse dies. People often think that if one partner dies, jointly owned property automatically becomes the property of the remaining partner and therefore isn't taxed. It's the other way around. Jointly held property is considered wholly owned by the first spouse who dies and all of it, not just half, is taxed. Ownership does usually pass to the surviving spouse, but not in all cases. It depends on state laws and whether or not the couple had minor children.

The only way to prevent taxation of jointly owned property is for the survivor to prove she or he paid part of the cost. This means that you must keep good records of any of your money which goes into jointly held property and investments. Don't just take your salary and buy stocks or whatever because the law assumes that your husband paid for everything. Unless you can prove differently, the whole thing will be taxed.

Insurance

Another thing that is considered the husband's property is his insurance policies. A wife may be beneficiary but unless you've taken legal steps to make the policies yours, the government includes them in the list of assets it taxes. As I said in the chapter which includes insurance, a wife should own her husband's life insurance policies.

Taxes for the Remaining Spouse

When the remaining spouse dies, there's no big marital deduction, nor half a home deduction. Without careful planning, the estate can be drastically depleted at that time. The new tax law in effect made the financial situation easier for a widow or widower but made it more difficult to pass assets to children or other heirs.

Capital Gains

The new law greatly increased capital gains taxes on appreciated property. It exempts $10,000 worth of household goods and personal effects from the capital gains tax, but everything else will be taxed when it passes to the heir. The tax will apply to any profit made on the holding either from (1) the time it was bought or (2) the fair market value on December 31, 1976. "Fair market value" means how much it was worth, how much you could have sold it for, on that date.

Keep systematic records of the original cost of your holdings and the date you acquired them. If you don't, you can imagine what a mess it will be to figure capital gains tax on an estate. Suppose you own six stocks, three pieces of real estate, and some municipal bonds. If you don't keep records, somebody is going to have to dig into your files and find out when you bought each asset and how much you paid. If it was purchased before December 31, 1976, he or she will have to figure out how much it was worth at that time, whether it was more or less than the purchase price. Then she will have to figure the profit.

U.S. News and World Report magazine gave the following real estate example to show how costly and complex the rule can be.

Jones bought a house in 1971 for $50,000. He dies 15 years later, in 1986, and his heirs promptly sell the house for $150,000. Suppose that, because of the size of Jones's estate, an estate tax—figured at the minimum 30 percent rate—is payable on the $150,000. This costs the heirs $45,000.

In addition, the spread between the decedent's original cost ($50,000) and the sale price ($150,000), or $100,000, becomes subject to a capital gains formula. The term of Jones's ownership was 15 years, and the period prior to January 1, 1977, was five years—or one-third of the total time. Thus, one-third of the $100,000 appreciation, or $33,000, is added to the $50,000 cost—to reach an unadjusted tax basis of $83,000. Since the house was sold for $150,000, this means there is a taxable appreciation of $67,000. The 30 percent estate tax is applied, in turn, to the $67,000 to reach an adjustment figure of $20,000. The $20,000 is added to the $83,000—to reach a final tax basis of $103,000. Thus, $47,000 is subject to capital gains tax.

You can see the difficulties involved with the tougher tax. So get an attorney to advise you and keep very good records of your holdings.

TRUSTS

One of the best ways to conserve an estate in the past was with trusts. A trust is the transfer of property from the owner to a trustee who will manage the holdings and pay income from them as proscribed in the agreement. A typical living trust is one where a husband transfers property into a trust with the provision that income be paid to him and his wife until the death of one of them. Income then is paid to the survivor. When that person dies, income or perhaps the principal goes to the children.

The new tax law changed the trust picture but no one seems to know how much.

Undoubtedly there will be court cases for years to determine fine points and clarify meanings of the law. A prominent attorney returning from a session on the new tax law told me many of his clients were waiting so he could give them advice on their estates. He said his advice was going to be two words, "Spend it."

Any trust established before April 30, 1976, and not amended since, remains tax free when the owner dies.

New trusts are taxed when the beneficiary acquires ownership.

Advantages of Trusts

Even though the tax advantages of most trusts have been eliminated, you still may find them useful for other reasons. An elderly person may simply grow tired of handling her own properties and prefer to put them into trust so she won't have to worry about them anymore. Or a woman who was so involved in her career that she didn't have the time required to take care of her own investments and business affairs might put her money into trust.

You can set up trusts for minors or for dependents such as the mentally incompetent who will never be able to handle their own finances. Putting assets into trust for a minor child is probably the best way to provide for his or her financial future.

Some husbands set up trusts for their wives. I was at a dinner party and a widow whom I'll call Marie was mentioned. She had been widowed a couple of years before and she began behaving irrationally. She gave money away in wholesale lots to charities, relatives, friends, whoever. She was going through the estate as if she couldn't get rid of it fast enough.

After dinner one of the husbands sat down beside me and said he wanted me to promise him one thing. "If anything happens to me," he said, "don't let my wife behave like Marie."

I told him I didn't think he'd have to worry. His wife was a sensible woman, knowledgeable about financial affairs. But you never know how a person is going to react when she is bereaved. Many older widows who have relied solely on their husband's judgment about money find they don't know how to cope on their own. Like children who have always been told what to do, they haven't learned to think and make decisions for themselves. They tend to turn to whoever happens to be handy for advice. If they listen to the wrong persons, they can wipe out an estate within a year.

Kinds of Trusts

Trusts can include a variety of provisions. The two broad kinds are:

Revocable trusts—you can change the provisions if you choose or nullify the trust entirely.

Irrevocable trusts—once you've set it up, it can't be changed.

How to Establish a Trust

You can establish a trust at any time. If you put it in your will, it's called a testamentary trust and provides that a certain percentage of your estate will be set aside and managed for a particular individual or individuals.

Decide what you want to accomplish with a trust and then talk with your attorney about how to make it happen.

Who Manages a Trust?

The manager of a trust is called a trustee. It's best to name a bank trustee. You're more likely to have the money well managed than if you left it to the management of an individual. Besides there are many cases where a trust has been mishandled or stolen and an heir winds up penniless. If a bank employee absconds with trust money, the bank will restore funds.

UPDATE YOUR WILL

Once you've made your will, keep it updated. If you made it prior to November, 1976, you should check it with your attorney because the tax-law changes may have changed the premise on which you divided assets. The big $250,000 deduction for a spouse makes a major difference. If you've left holdings in trust as a tax shelter, you may want to change them.

Even without the new tax law, a will needs to be reviewed at intervals. It may be obsolete if you've moved from a state where it was drawn because:

1) The lawyer who drew it up may not have been familiar with the laws in the state where you live now. You should have a local lawyer check your will if you've moved.

2) The executor named in one state may not be acceptable in your current state.

3)   The executor named has died or is not as capable of invest-ment management as you once believed.

4)   The number of your children has increased or decreased.

5)   One or more of your children have become adults.

6)   You have become a grandparent, or your grandchildren have increased in number.

7)   One of your beneficiaries has died or his needs have changed.

8)   The witnesses to your signature on the will may not be avail-able.

9)   You have disposed of property that is specifically mentioned in your will.

10)   The value of your estate has risen or declined significantly.

EXECUTOR

An important part of a will is the naming of an executor. This is the person who executes the will, who sees that its provisions are carried out. People tend to name a spouse or other relative as execu-tor because they want to save money, or because they consider it an honor. Suppose you think it would be nice for your middle daughter to be executor. She's efficient, honest, and you know you could trust her to carry out your wishes to the letter.

But do her a favor. Don't name her executor.

You do no one a good turn by appointing her executor, especially if she's an amateur. It's a full-time occupation from morning till night. The duties of an executor were furnished by courtesy of the Fort Myers *News-Press,* Fort Myers, Florida, and reprinted here with their permission.

1. Locate your will and file it with the circuit court.
2. Arrange for an inventory of your safe deposit box.
3. Obtain death certificate or doctor's statement for insurance claim. (Sometimes, birth and marriage certificates are also necessary.)
4. Obtain life insurance claim forms, fill out, and submit with policy. Obtain proceeds for beneficiary and Form 712 for tax report.
5. Obtain Social Security burial allowance.
6. Check on veteran benefits.
7. Check Social Security benefits for survivors.
8. Check possible pension benefits.
9. Locate your bank accounts. Transfer funds to the account of your estate.
10. Make short-term investments of surplus funds.
11. Obtain from court permission for allowance for support of family.

12. Collect certificates for all stocks and bonds.
13. Determine names and addresses of all heirs, legatees, devisees, next of kin.
14. Assemble necessary documents for each parcel of real estate—deeds, abstracts, insurance policies.
15. Investigate status of any business interest owned.
16. Locate and make an inventory of automobiles, furniture, jewelry, other possessions.
17. Petition court for letters testamentary.
18. Have appraiser appointed by court. Furnish appraiser with the inventory.
19. Determine what debts exist. Mortgages? Life insurance loans? Bank loans? Auto loans? Settle these debts.
20. Publish legal notice on claims against the estate in a newspaper acceptable in court.
21. Pay current bills in order to maintain property in good condition for later disposal. These are bills for electricity, water, etc.
22. If necessary, oppose in court all incorrect or invalid claims against estate.
23. Set up bookkeeping records for estate. Keep records of all disbursements and receipts.
24. Arrange for collections of dividends and interest on estate's securities.
25. Examine all real estate. Determine condition, adequacy of insurance, status of taxes and assessments.
26. Collect rents on income-producing real estate. Make repairs. Obtain tenants. Pay real estate taxes. Maintain insurance. Arrange for electric, fuel, telephone, etc., service.
27. Review all investments and make necessary changes as prudence indicates.
28. Obtain audits and appraisals of books and records of any business interest.
29. Supervise family-owned business.
30. Prepare annual accounting.
31. Pay claims after six months have expired. Obtain receipts or vouchers for all bills and claims paid.
32. Compute value of estate and federal taxes. Prepare preliminary tax notices required by law.
33. Select valuation date for federal taxes.
34. Determine whether administrative expenses should be charged against income taxes or estate taxes. (More savings possible if correct decision is made.)
35. Prepare estate's income-tax return. Determine charitable, marital, other deductions.
36. Prepare last income-tax return of deceased.
37. Determine how funds will be raised to pay federal taxes. Pay them.

38. Pay personal property and real estate taxes on residence.
39. Obtain estate tax closing letter from IRS.
40. If audit by a government agency discloses a tax deficiency, determine whether to appeal or accept the ruling.
41. Prepare detailed final accounting that is aceptable to the court.
42. Obtain order of distribution from the court.
43. Arrange for transfer and re-registration of securities with transfer agents.
44. Pay bequests.
45. Obtain receipts from all beneficiaries.
46. Petition court for discharge of executor.

Even knowing all this, some people are going to name their relatives as executor, so they should remember one thing. Name the person "executor Without Bond." Two very important words, "without bond." Otherwise the executor has to post bond, amount varying with states, and the sum will be deducted from your estate.

The best executor is a bank official. In your will, simply name your bank as executor. The bank is much better set up to take care of necessary details, and the charge will be minimal considering the work involved. If you want a relative to be consulted about proceedings, name him or her "co-executor."

TALK WITH YOUR HEIRS

Talk your will over with your heirs. There's no reason to keep it secret. Heirs should know how they will be situated in case of your death. It may make a difference in their financial planning.

One of my clients complains that her husband won't discuss their holdings with her. His excuse is that he has to think about it all day and he doesn't want to go over it in his spare time. If anything happens, he tells her, the attorney, accountant, and insurance agent will tell her all she needs to know.

Part of that property is legally hers, although neither she nor her husband seems to consider it so. She might even want to make some changes in their estate plan if she knew what it was. At the very least, she should be informed.

Children too when they reach a responsible age should know what an estate consists of and what part of it will be theirs. Parents however sometimes think that if children knew how much they were going to inherit, they would take to profligate ways and live on their expectations. Children fear parents will think they're grasping if they speak of inheritances when actually they want their parents to enjoy the fruits of their labors as long as possible.

It usually works best for everyone if the estate is discussed and understood by all concerned.

STATE TAXES

Another thing you may want to consider, especially as you approach retirement age, is where you want to spend the rest of your life. Just as there are good states in which to live, there are good states, where taxes are concerned, in which to die. People don't move to Florida only for the climate.

State inheritance taxes vary. If you have a $200,000 estate with a normal marital deduction, taxes in California are $4,600. In Illinois they're $4,400; Indiana $4,330; Massachusetts $7,875; Michigan $5,300; Minnesota $6,280; Ohio $5,480; Pennsylvania $11,940; Wisconsin $8,660. Without the marital deduction, the taxes are higher.

If you want to know what the inheritance taxes are in your state, telephone the public library, the business section of the newspaper, or the local law library, if you have one.

PHRASES OFTEN USED IN WILLS

Your will, when it's drawn by an attorney, is going to include certain essential phrases. It may speed things up for you and the lawyer if you understand in advance what they mean.

1) "I hereby revoke all wills and codicils previously made by me." A codicil is an afterthought, and is added on to the will and signed separately, instead of having a whole new will drawn. You have changed your mind, let us say, and have decided to name your bank as executor rather than an individual member of your family. It hardly makes sense to draw a whole new will; your attorney simply adds on a codicil to this effect.

2) "I direct first that my executor shall pay all inheritance, estate, or other death taxes, all expenses of administration of my estate, and all legal claims against my estate." These firms' mortgage demands against your assets have to be paid, and then the residue can be distributed among your heirs. But how can your executor pay them if you state in your will that your heirs get their inheritance first, and everyone else is paid out of what is left, when there may be

nothing left? This is not possible, and could have the effect of causing your will to be declared invalid.

3) "If my executor shall fail, be unable, or cease for any reason whatever to act as executor hereunder I hereby appoint the following corporate executor." This is inserted when it is your desire to name an individual executor but you want a corporate executor to succeed him in the event that something should happen to that individual.

4) "My executor shall have the right to dispose of any or all of my assets." This phrase is used so that your executor will be sure to have enough cash to pay death taxes, costs of administration, and legal claims. However, if you do not want all of your assets sold, this phrase should be carefully reviewed with your attorney.

5) "If my wife shall predecease me, then my estate shall be distributed as follows." Years ago it was common for attorneys to draw one will for the husband and then have the wife sign a statement that she concurred with its provisions. The modern method is for an attorney to draw a will for each spouse. The provisions of the two wills are identical in most cases, except for the names of the testator, which is the husband in one will and the wife in the other.

6) "I give, devise and bequeath all of my property both real and personal, and wherever situated." "Devise" means to give real estate by will, and "bequeath" means to give personal property by will. "Wherever situated" is certainly an all-inclusive term. By this phrase you are willing, therefore, everything of which you die possessed.

Now just before you settle down to write your will, let's take time for a test.

QUIZ

1. What two things have to be paid first from an estate—discounting final arrangements?

Debts and taxes.

2. You say liquid funds are needed to pay debts and taxes. Then you say bank accounts may be frozen and safe deposit boxes sealed. Where are liquid funds supposed to come from?

One good place is life insurance. Most policies pay very soon after the policy holder's demise.

3. It seems to me the safest place for my will is in my safe deposit box. If I leave it home, somebody may read it.

If you keep your will in your safe deposit box, survivors may not get it until days after your death. What if you have special provisions in your will about disposal of your body? Some people even name their preferred pallbearers. What does it matter if someone reads your will?

4. How long does the federal government allow for payment of taxes?

Nine months.

5. If a man dies intestate and his children are self-supporting, doesn't his wife inherit everything?

That depends upon individual state laws. Many states divide the inheritance in half, giving half to the widow, half to the children, even if they're self-supporting.

6. My husband died recently. I am his second wife and we've been married 10 years. We had no children. He has two children from his first marriage. He left half his estate to me and the other half divided equally between the children. Now the former wife threatens to sue asking for part of the estate. She says she deserves it because she no longer receives alimony. Do you think she has a good case?

I wouldn't think so but it's impossible to say definitely one way or the other. She should have anticipated her alimony stopping when your husband died and protected herself by owning an insurance policy on his life.

7. Handwritten wills aren't valid in my state so I don't see why I should bother writing one.

If you go through the motions of writing a will, you will of necessity assemble all the information that the attorney needs when he writes the will. By doing so, you save the attorney time and yourself money.

8. I've tried to think of someone to be guardian for my children if anything should happen to me, and I find something wrong with every potential person.

It's unlikely that anyone would rear your children exactly as you will. But wouldn't you rather make the decision than leave it to the court who knows neither your children nor the potential guardians?

9. I own a cabin in the Rockies although I live in Kansas. How should I handle this in my will?

There are various ways. The easiest probably is to make it an outright gift to heirs. This is something you should discuss with your lawyer.

10. I want all my children and grandchildren to inherit equal parts of my estate, but I want my preferred bonds to go to my daughter. How can I work that out?

State in the will that you want each heir to inherit equally. State that you want your daughter to have the stock. Figure the value of the stock and consider it her inheritance, adding to it to make the portion equal if necessary. If the stock totals more than other heirs' portions, either distribute some of the stock to other heirs, or let her inherit more than the others.

11. I have a few heirlooms—nothing of great financial value but they mean something to the family. I know how I would like to dispose of them, but some of the children and grandchildren have told me they want particular things. They are not in all cases the persons I would have chosen to give particular items to. I don't know whether the others don't want them or whether they just haven't said anything.

Why don't you ask them? If you want to give your collection of children's books to your granddaughter but your niece has asked for them, ask your granddaughter if she wants them. She may be too shy or too polite to say so. Or she may not care for them. The more you clarify these details before your death, the happier heirs are likely to feel afterward, both toward you and each other.

12. When my mother died, my brother's wife went immediately to the house and took everything of value. I never had a chance to inherit anything.

You should have an estate sealed when a person dies. If you must immediately notify relatives of a death, and think they're likely to help themselves in an empty home, tell them the estate is sealed and anything removed from it after this time must be approved by the estate executor. Practically speaking, this may not be defensible legally but it's worth a try until the attorney actually can seal the home.

13. I've owned a farm the past 15 years. If I die, will my heirs have to pay capital gains taxes on the amount it has increased in value while I've owned it?

That depends upon whether or not it's a working farm. Tax laws are different for working farms and ranches. If you've used the farm only for recreation, your heirs will have to pay capital gains taxes.

14. I would like to set up trusts for my grandchildren but my attorney said to wait and see how the tax situation develops on trusts. Should I?

If you wanted to set up the trusts solely as a tax advantage, you may want to wait until the 1976 law is clarified. If you want inheritances to your grandchildren to be in trust anyway, you can go ahead and set up the trusts. You may want to talk with a lawyer who specializes in taxes, if your present attorney doesn't.

15. I didn't know an estate executor had so many things to do. Even so, I know my son will be hurt if I don't name him executor.

Maybe he would settle for co-executor. This would give him status but save him a great deal of work. Banks are set up to handle executor duties much better than individuals are.

16. I've always admired Calvin Coolidge for speaking so succinctly. Can I write a one-sentence will?

Yes. But remember President Coolidge didn't have the tax laws that we do. You may find it more advantageous to your heirs to write a longer will.

One Last Thought

This book has been a pleasure for me to put together. I hope you've found it a pleasure to read. Originally I wanted to give you a guideline to financial security. Now I hope the book has done more: I hope it has inspired you with the will to act, to take your own road to responsibility in money matters.

Because ultimately you are the one who has to make it happen. You're the person who can turn the possibility into reality. You're the only person in the whole world who can make yourself financially secure. This dream cherished through the centuries by thinking members of our sex finally is a possibility. You have the power to make it fact.

I wish you a balanced checkbook, profitable investments, and a secure financial future.

M.E.S.

Index

abandonment, 136, 137
alimony, 140–41, 195
  escalation clause, 140–41, 146
  for husbands, 144
alimony trust, 141
American Council on Life Insurance, 70
Annual Percentage Rate (APR), 102, 110
  annuities, 77–78
  antiques, as investments, 52
  apartment complex:
    as investment, 59–60
    as tax shelter, 86
art, as investment, 52–53
auto insurance, 168–69

bankruptcy, 93, 125
banks, 97–102
  borrowing from, 90, 93, 94–95
  choice of, 97–102
  free checking, 97–98, 99
  free checks, 99
  free safe deposit boxes, 100
  loan officers, 94, 95, 106–7
  See also Checking accounts; Savings accounts
Barron's, 42
Best's Insurance Reports—Life/Health, 75, 76, 82
Blue Cross, 82

bonds. *See* Corporate bonds; Government securities; Municipal bonds; Treasuries
broker:
  choosing and dealing with, 42–44, 63
  commissions of, 43
  as investment-club adviser, 52
  research facilities of, 43, 47, 52
budgeting:
  apartment, 26
  car and car pools, 26
  debt handling, 125–26, 130
  extra income, 126
  investments, 25, 28, 120
  living at home, 26
  mortality rate of, 117–20
  overspending, 122–25, 127, 128–29
  preparation of, 117–22
  salaries combined or divided in, 116–17, 128
  for unexpected events, 120
Burkhalter, William E., 168

capital gains and capital-gains taxes:
  on bonds, 50–51
  in divorce, 139, 141
  on estate, 187
  on house sale, 162–63, 174
  on stocks, 63
Carnegie, Andrew, 53

cars, 26, 164–65
  choice of, 165–66
  cost of, 165
  depreciation on, 165
  foreign, 167
  insurance, 168–69
  maintenance courses, 170–72
  quizzes, 174
  resale value, 167–68
  service and repairs, 170
  taxes, 167
  trade-ins, 168
  used, 167
cattle feeding and breeding, as tax
    shelter, 86
Certificates of Deposit (CD's), 34,
    62–63
charge accounts, 90, 95–96, 97,
    129–30, 137
  mistakes on, 96–97, 137
  See also Credit cards
checking accounts:
  free, 97–98, 99
  free checks in, 99
  free mailing, 99
  joint, 3, 4, 100–1, 109
  minimum balance, 97, 98
  regular, 97, 98, 99
  special, 97, 98
  time lapse on deposits in, 99
child custody and child support, 139,
    140, 146
coins, as investments, 52
collection agencies, 130
community-property states, 94–95,
    107, 114, 139, 140, 177
component depreciation, 59
composite depreciation, 59
condominiums, 152, 153, 155, 156,
    157–58, 173
  insurance for, 162
Consumer Reports, 165
convertible bonds, 51
Coolidge, Calvin, 184–85, 197
Coolidge, Grace, 185
co-op apartments, 152, 155
Cooper, Alice, 114
corporate bonds, 4, 49–51
  call feature, 51
  capital gains on, 50–51
  capital losses on, 51
  convertible, 51
  current yields, 50
  discount, 50
  interest rates, 50
  maturities, 50
  rating of, 49
  trading in, 49
  yield to maturity on, 50
Cox, Orville I., 61, 85
credit, 89–93
  establishment of, 3, 4, 89, 109
  importance of, 89–90
  quiz, 108–11
  sources of, 3, 4
credit bureaus, 91, 96, 110
credit cards, 106
  joint, 3, 4, 109, 145
  loans on, 103
  oil company, 97, 137
  See also Charge accounts
credit rating:
  checking of, 91, 110
  establishment of, 93–96, 137
  negative, 91–93, 110
credit unions, 103

Davidson, Tom Q., 69
debt, handling of, 125–26, 130
depreciation, 64
  on car, 165
  component, 59
  composite, 59
disability insurance, 80, 81, 148, 172
divorce and divorcées:
  advice for, 136–37, 141–42
  alimony, 140, 141, 146, 195
  child custody and child support,
    139, 140, 146
  do-it-yourself, 143
  expense of, 139–40, 146
  fault, 143–44
  lump-sum settlement, 140, 142, 146
  no-fault, 143–44
  quiz, 145–46
  residency requirements, 144
  rights of, 145
  variance of state laws, 139

documents, master list of, 131–35
  to keep at home, 132, 133, 194–95
  to keep in safe deposit box, 131–32
  updating of, 133, 134

Equal Credit Opportunity Act, 90, 95,
    105, 109
estates:
  ancillary administration of, 181
  cash problems of, 176–77
  joint property in, 186
  preservation of, 70, 138
  probate of, 138, 181
  quiz, 194–97
  sealing of, 184, 196
  taxes on, 70, 176–77, 185–87, 193,
    194, 197
  See also Retirement planning;
    Trusts; Wills
executor:
  duties of, 190–92, 193–94, 197
  "without bond" clause, 192

"Fannie Mae" bonds, 38
Federal Home Loan Bank bonds, 38
Federal Housing Administration, 38
Federal Land Bank bonds, 38
Federal National Mortgage Associa-
    tion (Fannie Mae) bonds, 38
Fields, W. C., 101
finance companies, 103, 110
financial goals and planning, 7–8,
    30–32
  for estate building, 30–32
  in marriage, 113, 115–16
  realistic, 128
  for single woman, 149–51, 172
  updating and annual review, 117
  See also Budgeting; Investments;
    Retirement planning
Fort Myers News-Press, 190

gems, as investments, 53
"Ginnie Mae" bonds, 38–39
Government National Mortgage Asso-
    ciation (Ginnie Mae) bonds,
    38–39
government securities, 4
  agency bonds, 38–39

Treasuries, 34–38

health insurance, 79–82
  basic policy, 79–80
  for children, 82
  disability, 80, 81
  extended benefits, 82
  group, 81–82
  for homemakers, 82
  major medical, 80–81
  pregnancy coverage, 82
  from private companies, 82
  for single women, 148, 172
homes, 151–61
  advantage of, 156–57
  apartment as alternative, 151
  boarding houses, 151
  budgeting for, 153–56
  capital gains tax on sale of, 162–63,
    174
  condominiums, 152, 153, 155
  co-op apartments, 152, 155
  costs of, 152, 153–54, 173
  down payment, 155–56
  as investment, 151
  location of, 152, 153
  mobile homes, 151, 152
  property and school taxes, 153, 154
  repossession bargains, 159
  shopping for, 158–59
  tax advantages of, 156–57, 173
  townhouses, 152, 155, 159, 173
  when to sell, 163–64
  See also Mortgages
homeowners insurance, 132, 133, 154,
    161–62, 173–74
house renovation, as investment, 61
Hughes, Howard, 180

income tax:
  planning for, 85
  and tax shelters, 87, 88
  See also Estates
Individual Retirement Account
    (IRA), 66, 67, 148
  contribution limitations, 67
  savings account compared to, 83,
    88
  as tax shelter, 67, 83, 86, 88

inflation, 32, 45, 62
insurance. *See* Annuities; Auto insurance; Disability insurance; Health insurance; Homeowners insurance; Life insurance
interest and interest rates:
   on bonds, 49–51
   on CD's, 34, 62–63
   compounding of, 29, 31, 34, 62
   eroded by inflation, 32–33
   as factor of maturity date, 34, 50
   on IRAs, 83
   on Keogh plans, 83
   on loans, 102
   on savings accounts, 33, 62, 83
   on Treasuries, 35, 36, 63
investment clubs, 51–52, 64
investments, 29–65
   antiques, 52
   art, 52–53
   budgeting for, 25, 28, 147–48
   coins, 52
   compound interest in, 29, 31, 32
   conservative, 32–39
   in estate, 116
   gems, 53
   as habit, 40
   kinds of, 3, 4
   long-term nature of, 41
   paintings, 52–53
   portfolio balance in, 40
   prints, 53
   quiz, 62–65
   stamps, 52
   See also Certificates of Deposit; Corporate bonds; Government securities; municipal bonds; Mutual funds; Real estate; Stocks; Treasuries
IRA. *See* Individual Retirement Account

jobs and work, 9–28
   ambition and, 10
   aptitude tests, 11
   business travel and entertainment, 21, 25
   charitable activities and, 17
   competition in, 22
   deferred salary plans, 25
   do's and don't's, 13–14
   employer relations, 17–18
   employment agencies, 11
   entry positions, 11
   executive positions, 15, 20–23, 28
   expansion as means of promotion, 14–17, 27
   goals, in, 9–10
   high-paying, 22
   interview techniques, 12
   low-paying, 22
   nursing, 12
   pension plans, 25
   perks, 25
   and personality, 10–11
   promotion and job changes, 20–21, 27–28
   public relations, 12, 16
   quizzes, 22–23, 26–28
   salary budgeting, 25–26, 28
   salary negotiations, 12–13, 17–20, 27
   sales, 10, 12, 27
   secretarial, 11, 12, 21
   self-employment, 23–24, 28
   and social life, 11, 13, 21
   tax shelters, 25
   time scheduling, 24–25, 26
   training courses, 21
   visibility strategies, 17
   work habits, 13–14, 17
joint accounts:
   avoidance of, 100–1
   and marital separation, 101
joint ownership, 141, 186
Joint Special Committee on Life Insurance Costs, 75

Kelly Auto Market Report (Blue Book), 167
Keogh accounts and plans, 66, 67–68
   contribution limitations, 67
   savings account compared to, 83, 88
   as tax shelter, 66, 67–68, 83, 86, 88

legal name, 93
Letter of Intent, 183–84

life insurance, 68–77, 78–79
 agents, 76, 84
 amount needed, 69, 70, 83
 buying advice, 70–71
 cash values, 74–75, 77, 83
 for children, 72, 84
 collecting on, 79
 costs of, 75, 84
 for debts, 77
 for divorced women, 72
 endowment, 77
 as forced savings, 69, 83
 group, 78
 on husband, 137
 index numbers, 75
 as investment, 75, 83, 84
 loans on, 103
 for married women, 71–72
 for mortgage, 77, 162
 mutual companies, 75
 as part of estate, 3, 4, 71
 policy ownership, 71
 pros and cons of, 68–69, 79
 refusal of, 73
 safekeeping of policies, 78–79, 132, 134
 for single women, 70, 148–49
 stock companies, 75
 straight-life, 74–75, 76, 83, 84
 term, 73–74, 76, 77, 83, 84
 term riders, 76–77
 updating of, 72–73
 when to buy, 71
 whole-life, 74–75, 76, 83, 84
 for women, 69–70, 71–72
living together, 112–13, 114, 178
 See also Marriage
loans:
 Annual Percentage Rate (APR) on, 102, 110
 from banks, 90, 93, 94–95, 102, 103
 choice of, 102–5
 collateral on, 94
 consumer installment, 103–4
 co-signing of, 107, 127
 on credit cards, 103
 from credit unions, 103
 default on, 104
 early repayment of, 104, 108
 from finance companies, 103, 110

installment payments, 105–6
 from insurance companies, 103, 104
 interest variable, 102
 passbook, 104
 penalty for early repayment, 104, 108
 reserve checking, 105
 from savings and loan companies, 102, 103
 secured, 104
 shopping for, 102–3, 110
 women's problems with, 106–7
lump-sum settlements, 140, 141–42, 146

marriage, 112–30
 contracts, 114, 128
 as financial legal contract, 6, 113, 114
 financial planning in, 112–30
 quiz, 128–30
 separate credit advised in, 90–91, 110–11
 spending vs. saving in, 113
 See also Budgeting; Financial goals
Marvin, Lee, 114
Medicare, 81
Moody's Investment Service, 49
mortgages, 105, 111, 173, 174
 insurance, 77, 78, 162
 second, 159, 173
 sources of, 160–61
movie production, as tax shelter, 86, 88
municipal bonds, 3–4
mutual funds, 47–49
 advantages of, 48, 49, 64
 defined, 47–48
 growth, 48
 income, 48
 prospectus for, 48, 49
 savings accounts compared with, 33
 systematic investment stressed, 48–49

National Association of Investment Clubs, 51
New York Times, 42

Official Used Car Guide, 167
oil and gas drilling, as tax shelters, 86,
   87

paintings, as investments, 52
passport, 132, 133
pension plans, 68, 83, 86, 88
P/E ratio, 45–46
power of attorney, 127, 130, 132
pre-nuptial agreements, 114, 128, 137
price-earnings ratio, 45–46
prime rate, 34, 176
prints, as investments, 53
probate, 138, 181
   See also Estate; Will
profit-sharing plans, 68, 86

quizzes:
   cars, 174
   credit, 108–11
   divorce, 145–46
   executive characteristics, 22–23
   financial planning, 171–74
   insurance, 83–84
   investments, 62–65
   jobs and work, 26–28
   marriage and financial goals,
      128–30
   overall financial knowledge, 3–4
   retirement planning, 83
   single women, 171–74
   tax shelters, 87–88
   widowhood, 145
   wills, 194–97

real estate, 4, 53–64
   advantages of, 53–54
   apartment complexes, 59–60
   appraisal of, 134
   as best investment, 53
   on borrowed capital, 54–55, 57, 64
   buying advice, 55, 57, 64
   depreciation on, 59, 64
   diversified portfolio, 61–62
   example, 56
   house renovation, 61
   leverage factor, 54–55
   profitability of, 54, 56
   realtors' services, 56–57
   return on, 53

safety of investment in, 53
selling advice, 57
shopping centers, 58
single house rental, 60–61, 64
for small investor, 53
syndicates, 61–62
tax advantages of, 53
as tax shelter, 58–61, 62
trading of, 59
in will, 181
retirement planning, 25, 29–65, 66–68
   at age 25, 31
   at age 35, 31
   at age 45, 31
   at age 55, 31
   compound interest in, 29, 31, 32
   continuity of, 29
   IRA in, 66, 67, 83
   Keogh plans in, 66, 67–68, 83
   pension plans, 68, 83
   profit-sharing plans, 68, 86
   quiz on, 83
   Social Security in, 30
   thrift plans, 68, 86
   See also Investments
Rockefeller, John D., 53

safe deposit boxes:
   documents to keep in, 131–32
   free, 100
   for insurance policy information,
      79
   joint, 138
   sealing and tagging of, 100, 176,
      194–95
savings accounts, 3, 4, 32–33
   advantages of, 33
   comparison of interest rates, 34
   disadvantages of, 33, 62
   inflation as erosive factor, 32, 62
   IRA compared with, 83, 88
   Keogh plan compared with, 83, 88
   mutual funds compared with, 33
   old and inactive, 101, 111
   safety of, 34
separate-property states, 114, 139, 140
shopping center, as investment, 58–59,
   61

single woman, financial planning for, 147–74
  budgeting, 148–49
  disability insurance, 148, 172
  goals for, 148–51, 172
  health insurance, 148, 172
  life insurance, 70, 148–49
  pensions for, 148
  quiz, 172–74
  retirement income for, 148
small business, as tax shelter, 86
Smith, Perry, 168
Social Security, 30, 81
  for widows, 138
Social Security Commission, 30
stamps, as investments, 52
Standard & Poor's bond ratings, 49
Standard & Poor's Stock Guide, 42
stocks, 3, 4, 39–47
  buying and selling strategies, 46–47, 63
  capital gains on, 63
  common, 45, 63
  computer, 40
  confirmations of purchases and sales, 43
  defined, 40
  dividend reinvestment, 46
  dividends as tax shelters, 86
  electronics, 40
  growth, 40, 44
  hunches about, 47
  income, 40–41
  information sources, 41–42, 47
  investment goals, 40
  judging potential investments, 44–47
  at net price, 43
  P/E ratio of, 45–46
  preferred, 44, 63
  safekeeping of, 44
  study necessary, 40, 47, 63
  in syndicate, 43
  taxes on, 47
  tips on, 47
  utility, 40
stock market, 39
straight-life insurance, 74–75, 76, 83, 84

Tax Reform Act of 1976, 47, 185
tax shelters, 86–88
  advice on, 87–88
  cattle feeding and breeding, 86, 87
  company pension plans, 68
  deductions, 87
  home as, 86, 88
  investigation of, 87–88, 89
  IRA as, 66, 67, 83, 86
  Keogh plan as, 66, 67–68, 83, 86
  movie production, 86, 88
  oil and gas drilling, 86, 87
  pension plans as, 68, 86, 88
  profit-sharing plans as, 68, 86
  quiz, 87–88
  real estate as, 57–61, 62
  risks in, 87–88
  small business as, 86–87
  stock dividends as, 86
  thrift plans as, 68, 86
term insurance, 73–74, 76, 77, 83, 84
thrift plans, 68, 86
time deposits. See Certificates of Deposit
Treasuries, 34–38, 63
  advantages of, 35
  bills, 35
  bonds, 35–36
  buying and selling, 36, 38, 63
  interest on, 35, 36, 63
  notes, 35
  quotations on, 37
  Series E bonds, 35
  Series H bonds, 35
  tax-exempt feature, 35
trusts, 187–89, 197
  advantages of, 188–89
  establishment of, 189
  irrevocable, 189
  revocable, 189
  taxation of, 188
  testamentary, 189
  trustee of, 189

U.S. News and World Report, 187

Wall Street Journal, 38, 42, 60
"Wall Street Week," 42
whole-life insurance, 74–75, 76, 83, 84

widows:
  advice for, 136–38, 145
  financial ignorance of, 5–6
will(s), 175–97
  attorney for, 185
  bequests taxed, 178
  chattel, 183
  children in, 177, 178, 180
  common-disaster clause, 181
  disinheritance in, 178, 185
  executor's duties, 190–92, 194, 197
  guardian in, 180, 195
  handwritten, 178–79, 184, 195
  of husband, 136
  importance of, 175–76
  line of inheritance in, 177
  liquid funds provisions, 176–77
  multiple, 180
  mutual, 3, 4
  out-of-state assets, 181, 196
  personal belongings, 183, 196
  phrases used in, 193–94
  quiz, 194–97
  real estate in, 181
  revocation clause in, 180
  safekeeping of, 3, 4, 132, 134, 194–95
  self-proving clause, 182
  statistics on, 175–76
  updating of, 189
  witnesses to, 184
  See also Estate
Wills of the U.S. Presidents, 184–85
work. See Jobs and work
Workmen's Compensation, 81
Wren, Mary, 40